Vicky Nichols

571-238-6373

D1525310

Vicky,
Enjoy! *May God bless*
you + your family.
Marcie Cramsey

Deep & Wide

Raising Children Deep in Jesus
and Wide in Influence

MARCIE D. CRAMSEY

WESTBOW
PRESS
A DIVISION OF THOMAS NELSON

WestBow Press books may be ordered through booksellers or by contacting:

WestBow Press
A Division of Thomas Nelson
1663 Liberty Drive
Bloomington, IN 47403
www.westbowpress.com
1-(866) 928-1240

ISBN: 978-1-4497-8496-6 (sc)
ISBN: 978-1-4497-8497-3 (hc)
ISBN: 978-1-4497-8495-9 (e)

Library of Congress Control Number: 2013902634

Printed in the United States of America

WestBow Press rev. date: 2/28/2013

Dedication

For Jesus Christ, who is my Savior, and my heavenly Father—without You, Lord, I am nothing. With You, I am a powerful tool in your hand. Thank you for allowing me to minister to many people at the leading and empowerment of Your Spirit.

For my husband, Dan—you are one of my biggest supporters. When I felt like I could not continue to write or find the time for this book, you encouraged me and prayed for me. I couldn't do ministry without you! You truly know how to love your wife as Jesus loves the church!

For my four children, Matthew, Ashleigh, Nicholas, and Scott—I love being your mom and friend. Each of you has been my biggest fan, and you have taught me much about being a godly parent. I love your hearts for God and seeing Him use you for His glory! You are my dream come true!

For my mother, Penny Sizemore—you gave me the example of a good mom to follow. You have prayed for me, believed in me, and financially helped support this endeavor. Thank you for your heart for God, your example to follow, and for your confidence in me. You're the best!

Acknowledgments

Thank you, WestBow Press, for giving me the chance to speak to a broader audience than that in my current sphere of influence. I am grateful for this opportunity to publish a book that has been passionately on my heart for over ten years. Each person I have worked with at WestBow has been a great encouragement to me.

Thank you, McLean Bible Church, for influencing me spiritually and equipping me to be the servant leader God intended me to be. Thank you for your time, effort, and being God's vessel that strengthened me in the Lord. In particular, thanks to LeAnn Smart, who saw a gift of leadership and passion for children in me. You gave me a chance to follow God's leading, and because of your confidence in me, I am where I am today, making an impact on children and their parents around me.

Thank You, Jesus, my one and only, my forever friend, and my persistent Savior; I am yours always. Thank You for having me, loving me unconditionally, and accepting me where I am but not leaving me there. I love You and forever will.

Contents

Introduction

The War for Our Children's Souls

Satan is evil. His dealings are always evil. He will never change. However, it seems that in these latter days, he is more blatant with his evil than ever—or maybe I am just more aware of it. One night, my family was watching *So You Think You Can Dance* on TV. The song by Lady GaGa, "Judas," was one of the songs being danced to by a young couple. I had no idea what the lyrics to the song were, and regrettably, we watched. In the performance, two dancers came out of Pandora's Box. As they danced to this song, I listened in horror as the lyrics rang out blasphemies: "Jesus is my virtue, and Judas is the demon I cling to." My heart sank!

There are times when I am overcome with oppression by the blatant evil of Satan! Sadly, in today's culture, children and teens listen to these songs along with many others that profane and disrespect not only God, but also parents, authority, and the sanctity of life. They listen to this without flinching because they have become accustomed to this way of life. They are hooded from God's truth because they are so steeped in sin's blinders.

Children as young as those in third grade are exposed to immoral sex, drugs, alcohol, revealing dress, disrespect for authority, and much more. At every turn, our children are exposed to constant evil on TV, in the theaters, in the books they read, in the video games they play, and even in Disney movies. The evil of this world is in their schools, neighborhoods, and many homes.

A parent at church asked me why it was important to teach the children in the fourth and fifth grades about how to fight depression, the subject of suicide, avoiding self-injury, developing emotional maturity, demons, the Devil, hell, and how to develop biblical purity. My response was, "If we don't help our children learn how to reach out to Jesus and combat the evil that they are exposed to with the truth of God's Word, be assured, Satan will certainly reach out to them and lure them into the evil he presents to them."

It saddens me that these issues are exposed to our children at such an early age. It is unfortunate that their childhoods are robbed from them and their innocence is being stripped. However, instead of sitting in our sadness, horror, and regret of it all, we must not ignore our culture. We must rise up and fight for the souls of our children. If Christians and parents don't reckon with this reality, they could lose their children to the Devil in the end. We have to be proactive, not passive. We are warriors in God's kingdom. We must enlist in this war!

There are some Christian young adults who walk away from Christ, while others serve Him with full vigor all their lives. I have often pondered what causes this difference. While I will not go into all the intricacies of this dilemma, I will ask you a question. If you knew the mandate that would insure your child's walk with God would be strong for the rest of his or her life, would you take the time to learn, grow in, and live it? I am aware that there are many variables to this subject matter. I also know that our children have free will and can and will make their own choices, but we must not allow this fact cripple us into giving up, stopping the fight, or simply relenting to their wills. We serve a God of great power! If we have accepted

Christ in our lives as our Savior, His Spirit inhabits us. This Spirit gives us great strength and weighty influence on our children, for we are not given a spirit of fear but of power.

I have seen many parents give up too soon on their children who have drifted away. They stop the influence they once had as they despaired in their children's poor choices. They place their children's free will higher than God's power to change them. This can manifest itself when parents say, "My child has free will; there isn't much I can do now" or "I did the best I could for them; it's their turn to step up." It is true that there is a time in our children's lives when they are more moldable and teachable, but no matter their age, we must not forget that we serve a God who is more powerful than all the evil impressed upon and even sought out by our children. At all turns and no matter what stage our children are in, we must take advantage of the teachable periods in their lives while they are ripe; we must tap into the wisdom and power of God that He has graciously and generously given us. It is time to rise up and invest in our children! It is time to charge forward and keep what the Devil wants to steal, kill, and destroy.

Knowledge of God is one of the most important growth points to nurture in our children's hearts. It is the *only* eternal gift we can give them. All else on this earth will pass away. Earth is not our home; eternity is. Making the intentional choice to live and rear our children in this paradigm is our only choice. It *is* our best choice! If we don't live here in our parenting, sadly, there is a time when our influence becomes dimmer as the years pass by, making it more difficult for our children to come to the truth.

I am not saying that if you have a distant, rebellious teenager that there is no hope for him or her. That would be a lie. There is always a chance for change through the power of our God. As long as our children live and breathe, there is always hope. Prayer is one of the most powerful tools that we often neglect in parenting. Prayer can bring the power of God down from heaven to earth and change the hearts of our teens. I know, because there was a time when my own mother thought all was completely lost for me as a teen. Nevertheless, in the darkest evil place of my life, God intervened and radically changed me. The power of prayer did it. The perseverance of my mother prevailed. Her relentless teaching communicated God's constant love for me. She, my grandmother, and a group of people at church met weekly and prayed for me. They did this for a number of years. I'm a testimony to those prayers. I would not be where I am today if these prayer warriors did not enlist in the battle for me.

We serve an all-powerful, awesome God! He is strong and mighty; He is completely able to combat the Devil at every angle he takes to keep our children from God's love. God has given us a mandate—a handbook on how to fight the ever-present evil that surrounds our children. The truth is found in His Word; the covering for sin has been supplied by the blood of His Son, Jesus Christ; and the power to overcome the evil one is sourced in the Holy Spirit, who indwells us when we accept Christ as our Savior. Through the Word, worship, and prayer, we find wisdom, strength, and protection. We have been freely given what is needed to fight the evil one. The problem lies in whether we will receive, tap into, and employ this gift that God has given us.

Raising children can be a challenging experience; yet it is also a rewarding and honorable role given to us by God. I believe with all my heart that its success relies on our willingness to submit to Him and give Him the reigns in our parenting. This book will teach you how to help your children grow in their relationship with you and ultimately with Jesus. You will learn how to go from being Mom and Dad to being mentors, coaches, and leaders so that you will have a lasting influence and impact on their souls, *even when they have left home.* This book will also teach you how to help your children be wide in their influence with others. It is easy today for kids to be influenced by their culture. With the culture being as evil as it is, it is essential that children are taught how to be the influencers, *not the influenced.* Being the influencer not only gives them opportunities to lead others to Jesus, but also is a matter of spiritual survival!

Just raising our children in Christian homes and going to church every Sunday does not insure that our children will have a deep love for Jesus and choose to follow Him all their lives. It is certainly a good start. Recently, a missionary visited one of the parenting small groups my husband and I taught. She came to give testimony of her mission trip. At the end of her testimony, a parent asked her what her parents did when she was growing up that gave her such a deep love for Jesus. She shared that her parents loved God, took their children to church, and made the resources available for them to grow spiritually. This is awesome, and I say, "Way to go, parents!"

As the missionary's reply continued, what struck me was what she wished for growing up. She said that while her parents were good Christians and faithful churchgoers, she wished they had spent more time intentionally teaching her and her siblings the Bible. She yearned for that time at home in the Word *with* her parents and her family as one unit. She believed that if she had that, her walk with God would have been stronger when she was younger. Now, thankfully, she is in ministry for the Lord and loves Him with a fervent love regardless of what she wished for as a child. God's grace abounds! I believe that her parents did exactly what they thought was right, but I also think her testimony has a valid point for parents to consider. *Being involved in our children's spiritual growth gives strength to their faith.*

I share this story with you not to condemn her parents. However, I earnestly stress that being a Christian parent is much more than just placing our children in good churches and Sunday school. There is a clear command from God in how we are to raise our children so that they will follow Him. This doesn't mean that if we do everything right, our children won't walk away from God, succumb to temptations, or go through trials. It does mean that when these times happen, children will have the tools to get themselves back on track if they so desire. They will have relationships with their parents that are deeper than the typical parent-child model so that when they are willing to return to the values they received from their parents, there is a relationship open to them. They will be bonded as spiritual brothers and sisters in Christ. This bond creates a strong pull toward home for wisdom when they need it.

I still go to my mother when I need spiritual counsel, and I am forty-seven years old! The strong relationship I had growing up developed the trust I needed to seek her counsel today. When God is in the center of the family and parents intentionally teach the Word, worship, and pray *with* their children, they become "a cord of three strands not quickly torn apart" (Ecclesiastes 4:12). Bodies are not just woven together, but souls are also connected. The soul is forever; the body is temporary. This eternal bond can only happen when our souls are woven together through that which is eternal: worshiping Jesus, reading the Word of God, praying to our Father, and nurturing our relationships with each other.

I believe fully in developing a healthy parent-child relationship using God's spiritual connection through His Word, giving Him praise, and communicating with Him in prayer. Once we can establish this foundation, our children can grow deep in Jesus and wide in influence. These three activities will strengthen their walk with God while they live amidst the evil in this world. Confidence in the power of their God and the love of their family will help them persevere while they fight the war of this sinful society.

Many years ago, when my oldest was two years old, my goal for parenting was twofold. First, I wanted my children and I to know each other well. My dream was to talk with them, share my life with them, and know what made them tick, help them learn, foster their growth, and encourage them to remain open to my influence and teaching. Second, I wanted them each to know Jesus and His love for them.

Jesus reached down and touched my life and healed me of the rejection I felt from my father. God became my Father at the time I had none. The one thing I wanted to do right was teach each of my children about the love of God and the salvation that was ready and waiting for them through Jesus. There was nothing in this world that would stop me—nothing! Even all the good opportunities in this world would not thwart this plan. My husband and I have made sacrifices to meet these goals. We don't regret them; we rejoice over them. Our children are sanctified through their relationship with Jesus, and we are blessed to see them walking in the light.

When my children were young, I read the biography of Susanna Wesley, who had nineteen children, only ten of whom survived. One thing that inspired me was what was important to her: having a close, one-on-one relationship with each of her children and giving them each a close relationship with God. I figured if she can accomplish this with so many children, there was no excuse for not doing so with my four children.

The power of a person's testimony is healing. Hearing how God intervened and radically changed another's life invigorates the soul and gives new life and strength for one to go on. You will read many of my own experiences and how God reached down, taught me, and grew me as a parent. I hope that each testimony will encourage you, strengthen you, and give you a new hope to press on in this amazing venture you have undertaken: raising children for the Lord.

This book will reveal my passion. I get pretty excited over this topic! Jesus and children make me jump! I love them both. But I also love you and your children. My love for children and parents is one of the main reasons I am writing this book. God has put many parents and their children into my life to help and encourage. My heart has been given a special beat for each one. I put that heartbeat into writing so that more parents can be lifted up to the Lord and refocused on His power and glory instead of the futility of humanity. I want each parent who reads this book to know that he or she can have a powerful, influential relationship with his or her children. I believe that this relationship doesn't have to stop when a child turns eighteen! Are you ready to enter this war zone? Then arm yourselves, because we are about to enter the battle of various gods and find victory!

Deep in Jesus

Chapter One

The Victorious Parent

*Many of us suffer from temptations
from which we have no business to suffer.*
—Oswald Chambers

Driving from ballet to baseball, I sat at the red light, which seemed to take forever to turn green. Overwhelmed with all that I had to do that day, I laid my head on the steering wheel and said aloud, "How did I get myself into this state of constant busyness?"

My daughter of eight years at the time replied, "Because *no* is not a part of your vocabulary." It was as if the angels sang loudly, "Told you!"

In the introduction, I described an evil that most good, well-meaning parents shelter or at least try to keep from their children. However, there is another evil that tempts parents today. It is subtle. It appears to be good and profitable for our children. It is hard to escape at times. Its clutches clamp down tightly and demand servitude. Liberating ourselves from this temptation without guilt blighting us is like climbing up Mount Everest with lead rocks tied to our backs. The pull is strong, and the unwarranted regret dogs us if we don't partake of it in our lives. At this time in my life, I was grappling in the clutches of this tantalizing pull. Families of old can certainly relate.

Once Joshua took possession of the land that God had promised the Israelites, all the people took their own piece of the land and served the Lord throughout the lifetime of Joshua and the elders who outlived him. They saw great things performed by God in their lives, and they were in submission to His will. However,

> After that whole generation had been gathered to their ancestors, another generation grew up who knew neither the Lord nor what He had done for Israel. Then the Israelites did evil in the eyes of the Lord and served the Baals. They forsook the Lord, the God of their ancestors, who had brought them out of Egypt. They followed and worshiped various gods of the peoples around them. They aroused the Lord's anger because they forsook him and served Baal and the Ashtoreths. (Judges 2:6–13)

Somewhere from the line of ancestors and this new generation, God was forgotten in homes. He became a secondary thought and was reduced to a topic spoken of from time to time. And as time carried on, He became less and less declared until He was not discussed again. When God is removed from our homes, conversation, and hearts, the only alternative to follow is the culture and its various gods. And that is exactly what happened in this passage of Scripture.

We are born with a sinful nature, and if we do not walk the path of God's righteousness, we *will* walk the path of sin. Our culture is saturated with sin. Satan is deceptive; yet he presents himself as a camouflage of light, while darkness is his feed. He uses all at his disposal to distract and derail God's followers. His specialty is parents, because if he can deceive the parents, it is much easier for him to gain the hearts of their children and eventually their futures.

The key word in Judges 2:6–13 is *then.* Once God stopped being discussed, worshiped, revered, and followed, "then the Israelites did evil in the eyes of the Lord and served the Baals." It became easier for the Israelites to forsake the Lord and follow the various gods of the peoples around them.

Human nature has not changed or improved over the years, as some might think. Our sinful nature is the same. We still seek to please ourselves, look for opportunities to be larger than others (even God), and are in a constant battle for glory, which can sometimes be interpreted as finding our purpose. Even for Christians, this can be a great temptation. That is why whenever I receive a pat on the back or good feedback for something I have done for the Lord, I intentionally take the time to remember that all the good that people see in me is only because of all the good that God has placed in me. I remind myself often that "nothing good lives in me, that is, in my sinful nature" (Romans 7:18).

I am also reminded that while nothing good resides in my sinful nature, all the good I do have is availed to me from my generous Father, because "no good thing does God withhold from those whose walk is blameless" (Psalm 84:11). If we are to experience all the good that God wants to bestow on us, we need to submit to His ways of righteousness and mandate for living and desire the blameless walk He wants us to take. Often times the temptation for parents today is to walk in the success of *this* culture, be recognized as great among their peers, and be upheld by their own accomplishments (or their children's). These are held high by society but not by God.

Various Gods We Serve

Cultural influence surrounds us; it comes in the form of opportunity. The gods we serve are good, and they promise success, achievements, experiences, and positive self-esteem. Before we dive into what *we* face as various gods of our day, let's look back at what the Israelites battled in their day. What we find is a progression of what seems like the right decision driving them into the lethality of evil.

God's law is pretty rigid. Following God necessitates the gate to be small and the road to be narrow, and only few find it (Matthew 7:14). Few people take God's way seriously enough to practice and experience it. What determines whether we will walk through this gate is an issue of the heart. It is true that temptations taunt the body with fleshly delight, but the heart that desires them belittles the soul forever. This was the case for the Israelites in Judges.

The Israelites were captured—enticed, if you will—by the sexually unrestrained worship Baal offered. The permissiveness to go outside the proper limits of the law was probably intriguing, even freeing, especially if one feels restricted. Isn't that just like sin? At first it feels freeing and good, but then comes the hammer. Baal, the male divinity, and Ashtoreth, the female divinity, provided a temporary relief from this stress in the lives of the Jews, including all men and women. What seemed at first a temporary relief turned into bondage of the heart. Worshiping these gods elevated self and flesh while diminishing commitment and obedience. There was a sort of fabricated freedom found in this worship. It is easier for me to eat the forbidden brownie when I'm tired and stressed. On the other hand, I have greater self-control when I'm rested and refreshed. The Israelites were no different. They were under some stress in this passage, and that is one of the reasons they were easily swayed into temptation.

It is interesting to me that the name Baal means "master" or "owner." This is exactly what Satan's ultimate goal is—to master our souls, life choices, and direction. This bondage allows him to destroy everything we touch, teach, lead, and serve. A little sin in our lives leads to an ultimate mastery of evil in it. The Jews did not wipe out all of the Canaanite communities, as God had previously commanded, leaving their influence to infect the whole nation.

Much horror was required of Baal and Ashtoreth; Baal was the supposed giver of rain and demanded total worship in the forms of chanting, mourning, dancing, self-gashing, cutting, and immoral sexual practices that included orgies and copulating with animals. Ashtoreth expected women to sacrifice their morality by giving up their virginity, and they were to be the objects of these sexual atrocities demanded by Baal. Later, child sacrifice was practiced.

What is interesting about the fall of the Israelites is where they were in life when the temptation became apparent. Before Joshua and the elders died, the Israelites were nomads, and in this nomadic life, they were incredibly dependent upon God. They experienced His signs and wonders. They saw God provide for them in their desperate need for food and water. They experienced God's provision for family and generations to come. They had strong spiritual leaders who kept them on track. This, coupled with their walk with God, made for a close and intimate relationship with the Lord. These things made it easier for them to resist falling away from Him.

However, in Joshua 2:6, we find that the Israelites "went to take possession of the land, each to their own inheritance." In essence, they moved from nomadic life to being farmers of the land. This is a critical point in the life of their temptation. While their nomadic life entailed seeing great things God did as their provider and hearing of the signs and wonders that marked their ancestors' lives, suddenly the "wow" of God's activity turned into a patient waiting for His provision. God's "wow" is not always His woo. Certainly, Elijah learned this lesson in the cleft of the rock. He found God in the whisper, not the storm (1 Kings 19:12).

Often in this patient waiting for God, we discover His powerful whispers that alter the journey we travel. Often, the best part of our walk with God is the journey, not just the destination, because sanctification of the heart is in progress. Ultimately, in our waiting, we feel the pull of His woo.

Anyone who has ever planted a garden understands the patience needed for success. A farmer understands the surrendered dependence upon the weather's provision. Likewise, in raising children, surrendered patience is needed to develop them and see them through to the side God desires them to be on. Sometimes we misinterpret the period of waiting on God to mean God has become inactive. Then doubt sets in, which feeds distraction and ultimately feasts on desperation. Our desperation for activity then seeks a solution, leading to the sin of taking matters into our own hands. We see this progression in the Israelites as they follow what James says: "Each person is tempted when they are dragged away by their own evil desire and enticed. Then after desire has conceived, it gives birth to sin; and sin, when it is full-grown gives birth to death" (James 1:14–15).

Let us look at this progression as we summarize the spiritual state of the Israelites.

1. *The Israelites moved from being nomadic to being farmers.* Patience was required of the Israelites. Patience is not comfortable; if the discomfort becomes the focus, it brews into anxiety and displeasure. This displeasure skewed a paradigm for God's people, who saw Him as inactive. In reality, He was testing His people's commitment, dependence upon, and obedience to Him, as He does for us in quiet seasons.

2. *The Israelites' lack of patience turned to doubt of God's provision, and this doubt became their new companion.* Their doubt propelled them to seek a solution; they looked to their Canaanite neighbors and how they handled meeting their own needs. They contemplated their avenue instead of the route God gave them in His law; they were then in the clutches of temptation. Refreshing themselves with the Law and returning to God through prayer could have freed them, but they continued down this course of ruin.

3. *Doubt gave birth to desperation and began to fill their every thought.* On many occasions, the land experienced a drought, making food and water in short supply. I imagine that in these cases, the people's difficult circumstances rose above their belief in God's invincible power, making this change in focus the first of the various gods they served. At this point, they were dragged and enticed by their evil desire to seek a different solution than what God had to offer, which was faith in Him. The more they pondered their needs being met in a way contrary to God's ways, the less they thought about the danger of resisting God. Suddenly, the worship of Baal and Ashtoreth became appealing.

4. *Impatience leads to doubt, which leads to desperation, which leads to desire.* The clutches of temptation were clamped upon the people's hearts, and they engaged in the cultish worship. They hoped for relief from their stress to provide for their families. Sin took its full ride, and the Israelites became engrossed in sexual immorality, rejecting God's law, and rejecting His love and power to help them. This led to the death of God's provision for them and their relationship with Him. Leaving the canopy of God's love, they entered the peril of His wrath.

5. *The Israelites compromised their relationship with God and engaged in the sinful culture of the peoples around them.* They ended up compromising their relationship with each other. Marriages became defiled; children were sacrificed to customs that demoralized them. Men, women, and children were reduced to objects of use instead of people to cherish. *This is death at its best!*

Thousands of years later, our culture is not different from this one. We see on a daily basis marriages being defiled, children who are sacrificed to the ways of our culture, and men, women, and children who are objects of immoral use.

There is much to cover within this passage of Scripture, but our focus will be on how children are sacrificed to the ways of our culture, how parents serve various gods in our time, and how parents can be free from this wrenching evil that entices them.

How Did We Get Here?

A parent's desire for his or her children today is success in school, sports, extracurricular activities, relationships, college, etc. Success is the root. Is it a bad root? Not at all! Were food and water unreasonable needs for the Israelites? No. The need is not the problem unless the need becomes the god of our lives. If it becomes the god, we end up developing our own strategy to satisfy these needs.

Let's go back to my story at the beginning of this chapter. The temptation for me at the time was to give my children a plethora of experiences so they could find their niche. I believed the lie that if I did not offer these to my children, they would not be successful in life. For this season in my life, I was caught up in the clutches of this horrible temptation parents fall into. As I sat at the wheel, driving from ballet to baseball, the clutches began to clamp.

At the time, my oldest was ten. He was in baseball, my daughter was in dance, and my third child was in T-ball. They were in a home school co-op in addition to their home school studies. My oldest was also in a space program that met weekly; he was on the robotics team. I was a children's coordinator at our church, overseeing its K-5th grade program at one of its off-site campuses. I attended a women's Bible study while my children had study hall at the church. Obviously, I was a mom and wife. We lived with extended family, which in most cases meant more responsibility landed on me. My life was a bit out of kilter.

The problem with making success our only goal as parents is that we end up sacrificing rest, solitude, family life, relationships, sanity, and balance. At the get-go, I was sacrificing rest, one of God's wonderful commands. The fruit of rest and solitude is breathing. When we allow breathing room in our life, we are able to contemplate our relationships, choices, and vision for life. We can weed out the good and plant the best. I was missing this profitable fruit in my life, and it showed in my exasperation. The funny thing is, the busier you are, the more you pile on your plate and the less success you experience.

The lie I believed produced guilt if I considered not doing all of the activities presented to us. Everything we were involved in was good. Everything had merit and was profitable, but all of it together made life unbearable and marginal in its success. Less is always more. Less refines gifts, develops character, and ultimately brings the most success to life. The best part about less is it allows joy to accompany the success. Often we succumb to good things and put aside God's things. This is sin in its most deceptive form.

Marcie D. Cramsey

Throw Away the Foreign Gods

Joshua spoke to the Israelites before he passed from the earth into eternity with the Lord. He challenged the people to "serve the Lord with all faithfulness. Throw away the gods your ancestors worshiped ... and serve the Lord. But if serving the Lord seems un‐desirable to you, then choose for yourselves this day whom you will serve." He went on to state what he had chosen for himself and his own family: "we will serve the Lord" (Joshua 24:14–15).

I had a decision to make—serve God or serve the gods. I remem‐ber distinctly throwing away the gods of the culture by stripping our family's schedule to the bare necessities. For an entire season, we only had home, home school, and ministry on our agenda. I spent many mornings and sometimes afternoons studying God's Word and listening to Him in the stillness of my life. In this listening, I deter‐mined to only add to our agenda what I felt God calling us to, not what culture deemed important for us. I have held to this method for many years. However, having too much on my plate is always a temp‐tation. The act of throwing away the gods is a constant activity that I have to practice. They can easily creep back into our lives without warning or notice, because most activities are temptingly good.

In the process of stripping away the gods of our lives and dis‐cussing this with my husband, we both decided that our children were only going to be in one activity outside of home and school per season. And with this, only two children would be involved in an extracurricular activity per season. We have four children, so in the fall, two children were involved in activities outside school and home, and the other two supported and cheered them. In the spring, the other two had their turn; just as they did the supporting and cheer‐ing in the fall, the other two were to do the same for their siblings in the spring. Because I was in full-time ministry, I had to forfeit the woman's Bible study. My ministry team became my small group instead. Co-op was not necessary, so we dropped it.

With these decisions, order was brought back to our lives, and sanity was my new friend. To give my children a plethora of experiences without compromising my sanity, we allowed them over a couple of years to try different things, and then they were to pick the one or two things they wanted to perfect. My oldest picked baseball and playing the bass guitar. My daughter chose dance and writing. My third child stuck to basketball and music; he plays several instruments and sings. My youngest took up baseball and being a family comedian. (This he perfects every day, and we don't have to go anywhere!)

I have noticed over the years that our children liked some activities for a time and later dropped them and picked up others. Ultimately with this plan, we stopped the plethora of activities happening all at one time. My new goal was not success in all but success in one or two. But even these were not to compromise our family or time with the Lord. If any one of these activities began to derail us from these two most important objectives, they were either diminished or dismissed.

I have been in children's ministry for over twenty-five years. I have met many families over this time and have seen the good and bad decisions they each have made. I have seen some rise above the culture's temptations and experience the joy of following God's mandate in raising their family. Likewise, I have seen many families that have followed culture, just as the Israelites did. They left the canopy of God's love and lived under the perils of God's wrath. Observing this, I asked the question, "How did we get here, and how do we leave?"

We get here, because good things replace God's things. The way to escape these temptations and right our path is to go back to the Word of God. Reorienting our life to His truth orders our steps according to the Lord's direction. In Joshua's charge, he told the nation of Israel,

> Therefore be very firm about keeping and doing everything written in the book of the Torah of Moses and not turning aside from it either to the right or to the left. Then you won't become like those nations remaining among you. Don't even mention the name of their gods, let alone have people swear by them, serve them or worship them; but cling to ADONAI your God, as you have done to this day. (Joshua 23:6–8, CJB)

Our key words and phrases in this passage will right us to God's path of living. Let's take a closer look and discover how these concepts apply to our crazy, busy lives.

Our first key word is *firm.* The word *firm* means "to not yield when pressed." Being firm means focusing on the goal ahead that you are trying to reach. It means to be fixed, unaltered, and settled. Joshua told us that we are to be fixed, unaltered, settled, and not yielding to culture's demands when pressed and stressed. My personal goal in parenting my children was simple: to raise children who grew spiritually deep in Jesus and wide in influence. Their education and their activities pointed to that goal. This being our focus meant that anything that did not align itself with this goal was dismissed. The goal was not to raise scholarship-winning athletes, spelling bee wizards, or straight-A students. This does not say that high expectations in school were not important to us or mean that these successes were not welcomed. The difference was that all activities had to point to one goal: to raise children who grew spiritually deep in Jesus and wide in influence.

Our next key words are *keeping* and *doing.* Joshua challenged the Israelites to keep and do what was written in the Torah of Moses. We have sixty-six books in the Bible, and all of its truth is inspired by God for the useful purpose of "teaching, rebuking, correcting and training in righteousness, so that the child of God may be thoroughly equipped for every good work" (2 Timothy 3:16–17). Our mandate for success concerning our lives and the life of each of our children is found in Scripture. If any activity takes away from this useful tool to train up your child in God's Word, remove it. This is our priority as parents.

Our next key words are *then* and *won't become. Then* indicates the effect of a cause. This passage states that if you are firm and keep the words of the law, then you *won't become* like the nations around you. You will not follow the gods of culture; you will discern what God's goal for your life is, and you will understand clearly the futility of all the good that could deteriorate your walk with Him. You will know what to choose and what to stay clear of. You will have the wisdom and stamina to live out Joshua's choice for his family: "But for me and my house, we will serve the Lord."

Our next key word is *don't.* Don't mention, swear by, serve, or worship the gods of our culture. My family was watching *American Idol* recently, and a preview of Jennifer Lopez's music video was shown. As we began watching this, we all decided that it was time to turn off the TV! The video was a teaser to the full video they would be showing the following week. Collectively, we determined it was not for us to waste our time on. To be honest, we lost respect for Lopez and found it disheartening to see her dive into the depths of sensual evil. Its sensual and provocative focus was a modern-day worship of Ashtoreth, as so many of those videos are. That was easy to walk away from, but the harder temptation to fall into is the trap of doing too much.

Recently, my seventeen-year-old son signed up for a plethora of ministry opportunities at our church, and they were all happening consecutively in one weekend. I told him to pick the one he felt God was calling him to and dismiss the rest. It was a hard decision for him, as many people were counting on him, but if he had followed through with all those commitments, he would have ended up complaining and resenting ministry. I did not want to see that happen to him. He made the necessary calls to cancel some of his commitments and stuck with the one thing God had planned for him. I pointed him back to God and His purpose for my son, and this helped him be the most successful at what he was called to do. He could have done it all and done it all poorly, or he could choose to do one thing well and feel God's pleasure. In this situation, the *don't* meant he should not consider it all but consider the best one.

Our next key word is *cling.* When I hear that word, I melt in peace. The pace of my life falls in step with the Spirit of God when I cling to my Adonai! When my being, goals, daily activities, parenting, and direction are sourced from God's grace and purpose, I become saturated with His plan. I have the confidence, certainty, calm, and control needed to lead my children to their rightful destination that God has already ordained for them. Suddenly, culture looks inane, and pressing forward keeps me sane!

In two weeks, my husband and I will give our daughter away in marriage. This marks the beginning of the empty nest for us. A time like this can't help but cause us to reflect on our daughter's upbringing, scrutinize our faults, and celebrate our successes. My husband and I have prepared a toast for the reception.

There are many things I could say, such as, "I'm proud that my daughter graduated from high school home school at age fifteen. She will finish her bachelor's degree at Liberty University at age twenty. She is an accomplished dancer. She is an incredible leader of youth, a gifted young lady in the arts, and a hardworking, dependable employee." But that is not what I think about when I reflect on the success of raising Ashleigh.

In her home school and Liberty experience, Ashleigh sought to know the Lord and uses that knowledge to better her relationship with Him. Her dancing choreography was primarily used for churches and open-air outreach. Her purpose in this was to promote the gospel. Her leadership of youth has helped young girls overcome low self-esteem, bouts with depression, and self-injury; in this role, she has been able to help them find their value and hope in Christ. This is what I reflect on, and this is what I deem success! The other is icing on the cake, but certainly the core of all success is raising children deep in Jesus and wide in influence. If indeed this is the mark we have hit, praise God! We have won!

As I write this summary, I think of Paul and his letter to the Philippians on having no confidence in the flesh. He stated about himself that he had every reason to boast about the flesh, "circumcised on the eighth day, of the people of Israel, of the tribe of Benjamin, a Hebrew of Hebrews; in regard to the law, a Pharisee; as for zeal, persecuting the church; as for righteousness based on the law, faultless" (Philippians 3:4–6). He had every reason according to Jewish tradition to be called successful. But Paul considered all of it loss for the sake of Christ. In agreement with Paul, I hold to the same truth: "Everything else is worthless when compared with the priceless gain of knowing Christ Jesus as Lord. I have discarded everything else, counting it all as garbage, so that I may have Christ" (Philippians 3:8).

The various gods of this culture are very tempting. They are quite deceptive in their lure. But God is our strength, hope, and success. He is the only success in which we will find complete satisfaction. In Him, our children will soar like eagles, mount up under pressure, and win victoriously. God's success is lasting; the world's is passing.

Review and Reflection

1. What good things in your life replace God's things?
2. How do the choices you make in life resemble the Israelites' choices in Judges 2:6–13?
3. Using the key words used in this chapter from Joshua 23:6–8, map out a plan to right yourself with the Lord and allow Him to redirect your steps.
4. Read Psalm 16:4–9. What does going after the gods of our culture create, and what do these verses encourage us to do?
5. What do you hope to say about your child's accomplishments when he or she is grown?

Chapter Two

The Doorkeeper Parent

Earning a PhD (Praising Him Daily) contests the PhD in your prestigious university; while the latter commands a temporary rigorous schedule, the former develops steadfast, ongoing, lifelong character.

When my son, Matthew, was close to two and half years old, my daughter, Ashleigh, was born. While I had passion for Jesus and my heart beat for each of my children to know Him, I still had much to learn about being the parent God desired. While I loved Jesus, my Bible reading was sporadic at this time in my life. God wanted more of me, so in His plan to draw me closer to Him, He used my children—particularly, my daughter—to get me started.

Ashleigh was an easy baby in the sense that she slept well, didn't cry much, cooed, and was a very peaceful child. But the one thing she liked to do was wake up like clockwork at 5:30 every morning. I got up with her, fed her, and cooed with her each day. I was enamored by what God had created through my husband and me. Going back to sleep was not in the plan for a couple of hours, so as I laid her next to me on the couch, I began to think, *I could read my Bible during this time and earn my PHD (Praising Him Daily).* Thus began a fervent, consistent, vibrant relationship with my God. That was twenty years ago, and the relationship has not stopped since.

I was twenty-seven years old and had been a Christian for ten years by this time. My husband and I were faithful churchgoers; we were youth leaders, taught Sunday school to young married couples, and had a heart for following Jesus. We thought we both were at the height of our calling; we figured our relationship with God couldn't get better than this! But when children came along and it was time to teach *them* the Bible, I realized quickly that I had much to learn.

Being a busy young mom, I did not have much time for personal study. Soon after Ashleigh was born, along came Nicholas, and then shortly after that, we had our fourth, Scott. Life was busy, to say the least. But I was determined to keep my relationship with God growing no matter what. I wanted to make sure I taught my children, too. With the demands of motherhood upon me and the little time I had for myself, I chose to learn about God *with* my children! This decision turned out to be very important to the spiritual growth of my children.

One morning while Ashleigh was cooing beside me, John 10 clearly spoke to me. I saw a direct parallel to parenting and our role in this passage:

> Truly, truly, I say to you, he who does not enter by the door into the fold of the sheep, but climbs up some other way, he is a thief and a robber. But he who enters by the door is a shepherd of the sheep. To him the doorkeeper opens, and the sheep hear his voice, and he calls his own sheep by name and leads them out. When he puts forth all his own, he goes ahead of them, and the sheep follow him because they know his voice. A stranger they simply will not follow, but will flee from him,

because they do not know the voice of strangers. This figure of speech Jesus spoke to them, but they did not understand what those things were which He had been saying to them. So Jesus said to them again, "Truly, truly, I say to you, I am the door of the sheep." (John 10:1–7)

Good parents desire happiness and success for their children. In our society, you see parents investing money and time for their children's achievements. The appearance gives the notion that they care and love their children. Most do. This is one of the ways they show their love. However, the motive of parents helps us get to the root of whether their money and time are invested with everlasting love or temporary, selfish devotion. The question we as parents need to ask ourselves when involving our children in the activities of this world is this: "Does our attempt to give our children happiness, success, and a future reap an eternal return or a momentary, fruitless advantage?"

John 10 says, "He who does not enter by the door into the fold of the sheep, but climbs up some other way, he is a thief and a robber." This passage contrasts between Jesus as our Shepherd and something else in Jesus' place. When reading this passage, we can easily draw the parallel between the sheep and our children. We must then ask ourselves, "Who are we allowing to be the shepherd of our children?" Is it sports, material possessions, keeping up with trends, money, success at all costs, good grades, or perfection in all? In other words, are we concerned with all that pertains to this world? Are these lord of our children? Are these things climbing into our children's lives? If these have become the prominent focus, they have the potential to steal, kill, and destroy our children (the adverse effect we desire). Our children become puppets in the Devil's hand.

I am not saying that these things are evil. There is absolutely nothing wrong with our children being successful in this life using these things and more. But if these hold the position above Christ, there is a grave problem. There was nothing in this world (good or bad) that was going to keep me from building a close, one-on-one relationship with my children and helping them build that same kind of relationship with God. If any one of these good things were robbing this goal from my children, then a new plan was put in place. Our objective on earth for our children is not to give them success by the world's standards but instead success by heavenly standards.

God has given us much to enjoy on earth. We should be grateful for what He has given us by benefiting from it. However, the things of this world are weak even if they appear strong. They are foolish even if they seem wise. God wants us to live among the weak and foolish and enjoy the life He has given us but use this life to illuminate His wisdom, strength, and power. We need to live with the paradigm to use the feeble of this world and exalt God's power and strength above and through it.

My oldest son, Matthew, loved baseball when he was young. Naturally, my husband and I signed him up to play. From the time he was four years old until his high school years, he played baseball. His father was often the coach. They spent time practicing and learning the game so that Matthew could play well. However, the primary goal in their time of practicing was to build a close, one-on-one relationship with each other. The goal was not for Matthew to be the best on the team but instead to be the best *he* could be. My husband, his father, was not looking to shine because of some great feats his son accomplished on the field. My husband's goals were to build confidence in his son, allow him to have fun at something he enjoyed, and teach him to be a positive influence on the field for others via his character, not just his skill. In the end, they developed a lasting relationship using the game of baseball.

Today, our son is twenty-two years old. He doesn't play baseball anymore; he has moved on to other things in life. His relationship with his dad is very strong, and whatever they do together, they have fun and enjoy each other's company. Relationship was the strength sought; baseball was the tool used. Baseball, being the weak thing of this world, was used to strengthen the strong purposes of God: a thriving relationship between son and father. This thriving relationship has given Dan, my husband, an opportunity to mentor Matthew in his adult life.

This was a positive example of using the weak things of this world to strengthen the eternally strong of heaven. Conversely, there is a negative example that I think is important to share, because it is often the example displayed in our culture. It is an example that I share not to condemn parents who might find themselves in this setting but to warn parents so that they can take a good, honest look at themselves and make the necessary changes to the better.

It was a rainy night at one of the baseball games Matthew was playing. He was on a junior high team. Over the course of this season, my husband and I experienced a sad relationship forming on the team between a dad and his son, and it came to a head that evening. The kids on this team were good players, and many were skilled at different positions. But some who played well played for themselves, not for the good of the team. In some cases, their parents looked for glory through their kids' successes. You see this all the time today: Mom and Dad live their youthful lives through their children instead of assisting their children to be who *they* were born to be.

This particular father (one of the assistant coaches) was very hard on his son. His son held the position of pitcher. He had pitched (in the rain) the entire game. The team was losing horribly. His son's pitching was poor that evening; as a result, he walked a lot of players. His son was getting tired, and it showed in the poor pitching. I overheard the conversation between this son and his father about the middle of the game. His father wanted him to continue to pitch, but his son kept telling him that his arm hurt and that he needed a break. He wanted his father to pick another player to step in. There were others on the team who had the same skill and could have given this boy a break, but his father yelled at him and insisted that he continue to pitch and pitch better. The son was angry; he cursed his dad, went back out into the field, and continued pitching poorly. The team ended up losing the game.

I was so upset by this situation that I ended up talking to the father later that week. I shared with him my concern for him and his son. Actually, his conversation with his son upset the entire team of boys, including our son, so much that his outburst of anger caused many on the team to not want to play baseball anymore. The father shared with me that baseball was over for his son. I found out that his son decided he never wanted to play again. He now hated baseball. The father shared with me that his relationship with his son was also completely severed; he shared that his son also hated him. This was many years ago, and I don't know if any of this changed over time. I hope so. This saddened me very much.

This is a good example of a parent seeking success from the weak things of this world and losing that which is strong and eternal. This father entered the door of the sheep (his son's life) through the thieving glory of baseball. The growth of the son's character and the father-son relationship was not the goal. In the end, his son was not only robbed of his joy in playing baseball, but his father was also stripped of a timeless relationship with his son. I repeat the words of Jesus, an unchanging truth: "Truly, truly I say to you, he who does not enter by the door into the fold of the sheep, but climbs up some other way, he is a thief and a robber" (John 10:1).

What do these stories have to do with parents growing spiritually? And how does John 10:1-7 relate? First of all, regardless of how nice we are or how involved we are in our children's lives, we can easily lose our focus on what is really important. The only way to really stay focused on what matters eternally is if eternity is set in our hearts. What flows from our hearts comes out in our behavior. What we value personally will set the values we have for our children and their life goals. If relationships are important to us, then they will be important to our children. If material things are important to us, then they will be important to our children. If success at all costs is what we live by, our children will develop the same value.

As we continue in John 10, we must ask ourselves first if *we* are entering the door of the sheep through relationship or climbing in some other way. God created each of us to be relational with a deep need for intimate and close connections.

I know of a father who loves his children through taking them shopping. He believes that material things can make up for the lack of relationship he has had with them over the years. The funny thing is that if you ask his children if they feel loved by their father, they will both tell you that they do not. In too many cases such as this one, I have seen children be loved by their parents through materialism. In the end, they feel unloved; yet in this relationship, children end up developing an unhealthy infatuation for things—one of the enemies of love. Things are the only way these children know love, even though possessions never feed this unfulfilled hunger. The shopping temporarily satisfies while the heart's emptiness remains barren. The question now posed is this: how do we go from climbing into the heart of our children some other way to developing a relationship with them instead? We begin with our relationship with God and use this to instruct us with our children.

I reiterate John 10:2–5:

> But he who enters by the door is a shepherd of the sheep. To him the doorkeeper opens, and the sheep hear his voice, and he calls his own sheep by name and leads them out. When he puts forth all his own, he goes ahead of them, and the sheep follow him because they know his voice. A stranger they simply will not follow, but will flee from him, because they do not know the voice of strangers.

There are three types of characters in this the passage: the shepherd, the doorkeeper, and the sheep. These three are very important; if we don't define who they represent, we miss our opportunity to know how to be the parents God wants us to be.

Out of all three characters, the one that struck me the most was the doorkeeper. In some translations, this character is called a watchman, gatekeeper, or porter. When drawing parallels, the doorkeeper and the sheep can represent many kinds of people. They could represent a pastor and the congregation or a group leader and the group participants, but in our case, the doorkeeper represents the parent and the sheep our children. However, it is very clear in this passage *who* the shepherd is. In John 10:11, 14 Jesus told us that He is the Good Shepherd. No one else holds that role.

I find it interesting that the doorkeeper opens the door *to* the Shepherd. His role was to protect the sheep. He would not open the door to someone he did not know; he was confident that the shepherd was the true Shepherd. Notice that the doorkeeper opened something: the door. Jesus said in John 10:11 that He is the door and that anyone who enters through this door will be saved, go in and out of the sheepfold, and find pasture. Jesus is the person (good shepherd) and He is the door (the word of God). The true shepherd comforts and nourishes the sheep. He provides rest and safety. The sheep know the Shepherd's voice; they know it so well that they only follow Him. But interestingly, the doorkeeper has to also be intimate with the Shepherd in order to know whether to open the door or leave it closed when He arrives.

This brings me to the purpose of the parent. We are not the Shepherd; Jesus is. However, we are the doorkeepers. John 10:2 says that it is *to Him* that the doorkeeper opens the door. It is *to* Jesus that the door is opened, not *for* Jesus. *To* indicates that the doorkeeper is pointing the sheep in the direction of the Shepherd. *For* would represent leading Jesus to the sheep. Jesus already desires our children to be saved. He desires a relationship with them. He knows them, for He formed them in the womb. Parents open the door *to* Jesus so that their children will have the opportunity to choose Him, follow His voice, and live in His presence.

What a parent values will also be what his or her children value. Parents set in motion the direction their children will go. When parents make a relationship with Jesus a priority for their lives, they will also desire that same relationship for their children. In the end, though, loving Jesus is not a duty to perform on a list of things to do. It's not something we do because it is law. We love Jesus, because we know who He is and what He truly did for us on the cross.

I have heard many people say they did not feel loved by God. These are well-meaning Christians. Some seek wonder to feel blessed. They seek performance in the church and recognition. They go after prominent positions and work to make God smile upon them. The fact is that if the blood of Jesus is not enough to show us His incredible sacrificial love, nothing else will help us feel the love we need. Everything else fails, even in church ministry. When we seek something other than the blood of Jesus to feel loved by God, we trample the blood of the covenant under our feet.

This leads me to two other groups of characters mentioned in our passage of John 10: thieves and robbers. Historically, these represent the leaders of the Jews who harmed and used God's people. Jesus said about these thieves that they "come only to steal, and kill, and destroy" (John 10:10). The things of this world that I mentioned earlier can very much be like these thieves and robbers. Sports, material possessions, keeping up with trends, money, success at all costs, good grades, perfection in all, and other things rob the joy in life if held higher than Jesus, our Good Shepherd. They steal the relationship children can have with their parents and siblings, especially if they encompass all of our time. They can even kill children's original passion for the gifts God gave them, much like the baseball coach did for his son.

Because I minister to families, I have heard many a parent tell me they don't have time to teach their children the Bible. *They* don't even have time to spend with God each day. When their children reach the teenage years, the parents wonder what happened to their children. Suddenly the parents don't have the influence in their children's lives they had hoped to have. Their children care nothing for church or the Bible; they don't even believe that Jesus is real enough to help them. They don't have a proper understanding of sin, its consequences, or the hope of salvation that the blood of Christ brings them. Ultimately, the abundant life that Jesus has to offer them is stolen from them. All hope seems to have been killed. It saddens me to hear parents neglect the spiritual education of their children, because their time to truly make a difference in their child's life is ticking by. They are losing time and losing their children to this world.

I know this to be true, because I also counsel many teenage girls. Many have not felt loved by God. The girls come to me with plans of committing suicide and self-inflicted injuries scarring their bodies. They have given into the falsehood of this world as they try everything to please the demands of culture. They ended up hopeless and despaired. Thankfully, most of them thus far have come through with counseling. One of the most successful reasons they came through is that they learned how to love Jesus, trust Him, and lean on Him through prayer, worship, and the Word of God. While this was the primary reason for their success, the secondary and equally important was they learned to develop close, influential relationships with their parents. The counseling I give is not just for the teens, but also for the parents. If parents and children connect spiritually, a counselor has ultimately won the battle for the child in care.

The doorkeeper in John 10 is a vital role parents play in their children's lives. We end with a few questions to ponder. Do you value your own relationship with Jesus? Do you spend daily time with Him, getting to know your Savior intimately? Are you developing your own PHD (Praising Him Daily)?

Deuteronomy 6:7 commands parents to teach their children diligently. However, before that command, God gives parents a mandate in verses 4–6: "Hear, O Israel! The Lord is our God, the Lord is one! And you (parents) shall love the Lord your God with all your heart and with all your soul and with all your might. And these words, which I am commanding you today, shall be on your heart." Parents cannot possibly expect to have a spiritual impact on their children if no commitment to God marks their own lives. What parents value, their children value. What parents have in their hearts is what they can give to their children. If parents have a desire for worldly success, that is what they will give to their children. On the other hand, if God's Word is what they hold dear to their lives and hearts, that is what they will share with their children.

The word *heart* in this passage is quite impressive when we see the Hebrew definition. Loving God with all our hearts means to love Him in all of the activities of our lives: the inner soul, mind, will, conscience, courage, intelligence, and purpose.[1] The appetites of our lives and the whole of our beings love God. When we are infused with this kind of devotion to our God, our love for Him will automatically overflow into our children. It is as if we become a saturated sponge that spills into our children and others around us. Truly, "as water reflects the face, so one's life reflects the heart" (Proverbs 27:19).

In this loyalty, we will prioritize our lives around this display of devotion to all in our influence. God commanded this for a reason. If parents do not allow their own lives to show this kind of love for God, then Deuteronomy 6:7–9 will never be fully accomplished in their parenting. Don't be fooled and think that your children don't know what and who you truly cherish in your life. They can see much more in us than what we are willing to acknowledge for ourselves.

Deuteronomy 6:7–9 clearly states how we are to diligently open the door to our Good Shepherd and point our children to Him: "And you shall teach them diligently to your sons (and daughters) and shall talk of them when you sit in your house and when you walk by the way and when you lie down and when you rise up. And you shall bind them as a sign on your hand and they shall be as frontals (thoughts) on your forehead. And you shall write them on the doorposts of your house and on your gates."

Take note of the verbs in this passage: teach, talk, sit, walk, lie, rise, bind, think, and write. All of these actions open the door to Jesus for our children. All point our children *to* Him. They all encompass an entire way of life for them. They allow our children to see God in the whole of their world, not just in compartments. God should envelop our entire lives. The only way to make this happen fully is for it to fully be in each parent's heart. What parents value, their children will value. Proverbs 27:19 says, "As water reflects the face, so one's life reflects the heart."

We come to the end of this chapter to begin another. How do we actually teach, talk, sit, walk, lie, rise, bind, think, and write God's Word on the hearts of our children? We see value, but we must move to action, for value without action leads to aggravation, apathy, and abandonment. These are not the weapons we enter battle with; on the contrary, we enter battle with God's confidence, His power, and our involvement.

Reflection and Review

1. Explain how parents fill the role of doorkeepers.
2. In what ways do you point your children to Jesus? Do you allow other things to take His place in your life and your children's lives? What are they?
3. What testimony (story) shared in this chapter can you relate to? How?
4. Using the Hebrew definition of *heart,* how are you developing your love for God in these areas?
5. Read Ezekiel 34:1–5. The term shepherd in this passage can be used simultaneously with the term doorkeeper we find from John 10:3. How does the baseball dad in this chapter compare to the shepherds in the Ezekiel passage? In what ways does the baseball dad's son compare to God's people described? How does this type of leading hinder our influence on our children?
6. What is meant by the phrase, "What a parent values, his or her children will value"?

Chapter Three

The Teaching Parent

The difference between the school of knowledge
and the school of heart is that the former is of
the flesh, and the latter is of the Spirit.

Many years ago, when my children were very young, my good friend handed me a biography titled *Susanna Wesley: Servant of God* by Sandy Dengler and encouraged me to read it. She said that Susanna reminded her of me, particularly in how she taught her children spiritual truths and spent personal time with each of them. Intrigued and probably a bit narcissistic at the time, I got busy reading this book.

As I read this biography, I became quite humbled that my good friend thought I was anything like this amazing woman of God. Susanna birthed nineteen children and lost nine of them to death. She was married to a man whom she loved very much, but his spending problem made living very stressful, as they were constantly in debt. He traveled a lot, leaving Susanna home to take care of the children and at times the rectory, too. Susanna also experienced poor health as a result of her pregnancies. However, regardless of the trials and struggles this woman faced, she did not allow any of them to get in the way of her own study of God's Word, the spiritual or academic training of her children, or the close relationships she had with each child.

Two of Susanna's sons, John and Charles Wesley, were the co-founders of Methodism and leaders of the evangelical revival in the Church of England during the eighteenth century. Dengler writes what John Wesley said of his mother, "I learned more about Christianity from my mother than from all the theologians of England." *That*, my friend, is exactly what God has commanded a parent in Deuteronomy 6:4–9 to do!

Three things that truly amazed me about Susanna were her devotion to prayer, her dedication to studying God's Word, and the value she placed on developing personal relationships with her children. Regardless of their small abode or how many children surrounded her, Susanna would often cover her head with her apron and pray. Her children knew at that moment that their mother was spending time alone with the Lord, and they were not to disturb her. Prayer gave Susanna the strength to carry on; her relationship with God through the Word was also a priority. These were her personal commitments, and they overflowed into teaching the same to her children.

As noted by John Wesley's comment, each child received from Susanna intentional instruction from the Word of God. She was devoted to taking the time to nurture and feed them spiritually, not just physically and academically. Interestingly, the manner by which she imparted God's Word was through a relationship with each of her children. With ten children in her life, you may wonder how on earth she was able to spend that individual time. It was important to her. What is important to a person causes him or her to take the necessary measures to make it happen. It became her priority, so she would leave other seemingly important yet least imperative things in life at bay so that she could know her children individually.

Susanna desired to know each child—know what they thought, what they felt, and what made them tick—and from this relationship, she was able to raise children who loved and served God with their whole lives. She taught them how to have a relationship! She lived a life that imitated Christ; it was this life her children saw day after day. She was not perfect, and certainly she fought temptations of the flesh; she often had feelings inferior to the Spirit of God. But her hope was in the Lord. She righted herself to His Word and found refuge in His truth. Ultimately, her dedication to prayer and the Word caused her to discover a relationship with Jesus that warmed her heart far beyond what she ever imagined when she began this journey.

Susanna became a model for me to follow. It was important to me to imitate her as she had imitated Christ. Hebrews 6:12 encourages us to "…imitate those who through faith and patience inherit what has been promised." Susanna raised children who loved God. Likewise, I wanted to reap the same with my children. Hebrews 13:7 continues to instruct us, "Remember your leaders, who spoke the word of God to you. Consider the outcome of their way of life and imitate their faith." While I do not know Susanna personally, the story of her life became a teacher to me. It is important to imitate those around us (dead or alive) who imitated and imitate Jesus. We will therefore live lives that are worthy for others to emulate, particularly our children. Is your life worthy of imitation? Do your children follow behaviors and character traits that resemble Christ? Or does the world dictate their behavior? A word of caution—when a child's behavior and character traits are of poor value, we often need to look at those surrounding them, such as poorly influential friends, and believe it or not, even ourselves!

God's Mandate

Deuteronomy 6:5–6 specifically talks to parents. We know this by the statement "so that you, your children and their children after them." If God's Word is not on the hearts of parents, they cannot give it away to their children. If parents do not love the Lord their God with all *their* hearts, how can they impart that to their children? If God is not a part of *their* deep souls and *their* ever-present minds, then they cannot teach or make a spiritual impact on their children. The lives we live are what our children will imitate.

Susanna Wesley was a woman who valued personal study of theology (the study of God), and her avenue that accomplished this was her Bible. She was an intellectually accomplished woman; there were many Oxford men who didn't match up to her knowledge and insight. Sandy Dengler shares in *Susanna Wesley: Servant of God* one of Susanna's firm beliefs that helped her accomplish success in what she knew spiritually. "A regular and orderly day provides that nothing will be neglected. You might well feel more pious later, but keeping to a strict order ensures that you'll be pious, whether you feel like it or not. One must never trust whim and feeling."[2] She decided that her time with God was not going to be interfered with or altered for any reason.

When Susanna had her first son, Sam, she made the commitment that even with this precious child who had come into her life and needed much care, she "would not allow him to rob her of her daily study. If the reality of motherhood was constant busyness, she would master reality and bend it to her own iron will."[3] If all mothers today spoke to their busyness with such conviction, where would we and our children be in our walks with God? Often we bend to the wrong will and master the wrong urgencies!

Susanna's commitment may sound rigid, and it was, but it was more about her desperate devotion to God than rigidity. The fruit of her commitment was the spiritual wisdom she gave to her children. She stuck to it regardless of her feelings. This goes against American culture, for most do what they feel like, not what is right.

Susanna was not afraid to take up the baton and lead her children to God. I have heard many moms say to me, "The spiritual training is my husband's responsibility." Yes, this it is! However, this truth is not reason for a mother to neglect her responsibility to also teach her child about God. Proverbs 1:8 commands, "Listen, my son (and daughter), to your father's instruction and do not forsake your mother's teaching." Both parents are to be involved. And teaching is the most time-consuming of the two.

Instruction is simply that—instruction. Say it once, and obey it. But teaching takes coaching, walking with, and nurturing lesson upon lesson to insure that what is taught is learned. And who better to do this than the mom who spends the most time with the children? Take a look at Timothy in the New Testament. Who gave Timothy the spiritual wisdom he had? Paul tells us clearly that he was "reminded of Timothy's sincere faith, which first lived in his grandmother Lois and in his mother Eunice and, he was persuaded, now lived in Timothy also" (2 Timothy 1:5). Notice where the sincere faith lived first: in Timothy's grandmother and mother! Love for God has to start in the hearts of the parents before it can truly be given to the children.

History points out that Timothy's father was Greek and did not share the belief of his wife. Eunice could have said, "Oh well, too bad for Timothy." Many women use excuses to not teach their children God's truth. I believe they do this because God is ultimately not that important to them or they are not willing to give up something else in their life so they can do the right thing. Whatever the reason, not teaching our children God's Word is never His will for our children. That seems harsh; in essence, though, if we do not face the hard truth, we become complacent and neglectful of the chief parts of our parenting.

God has called me to speak truth to the hearts of parents, not just for encouragement, but also to challenge them. I like what Mark

Driscoll from Mars Hill Church in Seattle, Washington says: "Hard words produce soft people, but soft words produce hard people." It doesn't benefit God's kingdom for me to encourage a harder generation of parents to be even harder. How does this help our children today? In reality, if I am going to take the time to write a book, I'm going to take the time to write it in such a way that encourages radical change; our children are at stake if I don't.

Susanna Wesley did not always have her husband home to help her in the spiritual training of the children. But her dedication to God first enabled her to have the passion and fervor to do what was crucial for her children. Susanna's belief was noted in Dengler's biography. "The responsibility for the children's spiritual instruction was Sam's (her husband), but since he was not home she must be the one to discharge it."[4]

My husband has been faithful to instruct our children and encourage them to listen to their mother's teaching. He has also been faithful to work two jobs if necessary to allow me to be the stay-at-home mom that God called me to be. With his dedication to care for his family, he has also not been home much for the spiritual teaching of our children. When he could be there, he was, but when he couldn't, there was no way that I was going to neglect this imperative responsibility I had to my kids.

When my oldest, Matthew, was almost three years old and my daughter just a baby, I sat quietly in my living room while both were taking a nap. I read the book of Revelation in one sitting. What seemed like a hard book at first suddenly became very easy to understand! I do not have eschatology all figured out. It wasn't so much the end times and its specifics that God showed me that day; it was the purpose He had for each of my children.

I was enthralled with being a mom. I loved my children with

everything I had. I had also begun a consistent time with God during which I fell in love with Him more and more each day. Suddenly that day, God spoke to me clearly with an impression in my spirit that I will never forget. That impression from God was *I have not given you these children and the ones to come in the near future for just the purpose of enjoying them and loving them. I have also entrusted them to you so that you would raise them to be warriors in My kingdom. They are My servants, and you are the one to teach them about Me. You are to shepherd them like I shepherd you; you will care for them with the purpose of pointing them to Me.*

My spirit was overwhelmed with the responsibility. I knew that I could not do this alone; I needed God's Spirit every day so that I would complete His calling on my life. That day marked a new paradigm for motherhood for me. There would be nothing that interrupted what God had summoned me to do: teach my children to love Jesus, know Him personally, and serve Him with all their hearts!

My prayer after that day became consistent: "God, teach me so that I can teach them." And that is exactly what He has done. I have asked Him for wisdom, insight, understanding, and His plan every day forward. Currently, I face an empty nest, but I still pray the same prayer. It is never-ending! My influence may be different on my children at the adult stage of life than it was when they were young, but take note; there is no age limit given in Proverbs 1:8. My teaching and their Father's instruction is continuous. Its delivery, however, may take a different form.

Teaching that Engages the Soul

Our first step in imprinting God's faith and morals on our children starts with parents. We will now look at how to do this in a way that engages our children toward God not against Him. There are many approaches that we can take in teaching our children God's Word that result in a deep faith in God. Some approaches can discourage faith and affect our children dangerously in their walks with Him. We will look at the part that negatively affects woven within the ways that profit them in their faith.

We find our answers by taking a look at Deuteronomy 6:7–9 (NASB): "You shall teach them diligently to your sons and shall talk of them when you sit in your house and when you walk by the way and when you lie down and when you rise up. You shall bind them as a sign on your hand and they shall be as frontals on your forehead. You shall write them on the doorposts of your house and on your gates."

We will break this passage down in practical pieces and put feet to them in our daily lives. In Hebrew, the word *teach* is defined as "to whet, to pierce, to sharpen."[5] *Whet* is further defined as "to stimulate the appetite and the curiosity." These definitions give us clarity in what we are actually doing when we teach our children. There are three actions happening here, and they typically follow a certain order.

To Whet When it comes to teaching the Word of God to our children, we are to first stimulate their interests. When children are young, they love to hear stories. Taking a children's Bible with colorful, intriguing pictures; reading a story to them every night; talking about the pictures; and asking questions concerning the story elements stimulates interest. When the children get older and begin to read on their own, they go from being stimulated to developing an appetite for the truth. My children and I read together at this stage of teaching; they read parts of the story, and then I read parts, too. As they gained more confidence in their reading ability, we moved from children's Bible story books to a simple version of the Bible, such as New Century Version. This process gently increased their enjoyment of and curiosity about the Bible.

As my children and I read the stories, they became familiar with God's people and His natural involvement in their lives. This gave my children a sense of God's genuine and authentic involvement in their own lives. As they became elementary age, we added to our nightly reading and read morning devotions. This was a daily routine we did Monday through Friday. Like clockwork, Bible study started at 9:00 a.m. with a twenty- to forty-minute duration. The duration depended on the ages I was teaching and the attention span of my children at the time. This routine began our school day. (I homeschooled.) This study time gave us the proper lens to see our day, their academics, and our world.

One evening, my husband and I piled into our children's bedroom, and we read from Proverbs. We read a story that explained the proverb and then the verse itself. The story and the passage was so convicting to our son, Nicholas (four years old at the time), that he desperately wanted to accept Jesus into his heart. This gave us the wonderful opportunity to pray with him that evening! These story times are invaluable when it comes to leading our children to the Lord. That evening will always mark my heart with everlasting joy!

This story time did not just infuse a curiosity for God's Word, it also enabled the relationships we had with our children to grow. It gave us the opportunity to impart our beliefs, values, and convictions to them. Story times encourage dialogue, questions, understanding, and life change. They allow parents to get to know what their children think and supplement their thinking with what is needed. Children learn much with this consistency. Our time in the morning and our story time in the evening would liken the part of Deuteronomy: "You … shall talk of them when you sit in your house, when you lie down and when you get up."

To whet their appetite with curiosity is not the place to remain, though. As the children grow, we must dig deeper in their hearts and encourage God's Word to take root. Our second definition of teaching is to pierce.

To Pierce It is important to move from just reading stories to piercing the hearts of our children for Christ. This involves two very important elements: memorizing Scripture and making personal application. It is good to begin the spiritual education of our children with reading the stories of the Bible, familiarizing our children with God's people and His hand in their lives through the Word. But if we only read the stories as if they are just good literature, then we have missed the vision for the Word of God.

Second Timothy 3:16–17 gives us a very clear objective use for God's Word: "All Scripture is God-breathed and is useful for teaching, rebuking, correcting and training in righteousness, so that the servant of God may be thoroughly equipped for every good work." To pierce God's Word into the hearts of our children requires more than teaching, rebuking, and correcting. This alone can be damaging to a child's faith. Eventually, if a child only experiences the Word of God as judgment, he or she will resent the Word of God and never feel the love of God. In order for our children to be thoroughly equipped, we must also train. Training empowers; this empowerment includes memorization, meditation, practice, and seeing the *why* behind the *what* of the Bible. This lends itself easily to application.

If we only answer the *what* of the Bible, we run the risk of just engaging the mind. This is where memorization could take the wrong direction. Winning Bible bees is not the goal! In Matthew 22:37, Jesus quoted the Old Testament law, "You shall love the Lord your God with all your heart, with all your soul, and with all your mind." This was the greatest and foremost commandment.

Notice the sequence of what we are to love God with: heart, soul, and mind. This sequence is intentional and very important, as it singles out what Jesus wants from us most. If we just love God with our minds and for the sole purpose of gaining knowledge, we are not much different than the Pharisees. They knew the law well; their knowledge, however, puffed them up with pride, and they arrogantly led the people of Israel with tyranny instead of love. If we are not careful as parents, we can fall into this trap of leading our children the same way. Our children will grow up either legalistic, not knowing Christ's love, or feeling condemned by the law without understanding the freedom of grace.

Many children fall into the second category. When they become young adults, they walk away from the faith—a tragic decision in their lives that could have been avoided. I knew a mom who tucked her fourth-grade daughter in bed with a list of all her daughter's sins that day. Every night, her daughter had *that* horrible bedtime story to look forward to. Hearing this made me sick and very sad for this little girl.

When raising our children, my husband and I gave our children a set of rules that were to be obeyed. We didn't stop there; we then told them *why* they needed to obey them. The *why* engaged their hearts, and they were able to discern better the reasons behind the rule. This actually encouraged consistent obedience from our children. The same is true for their spiritual training. When we engage the hearts of our children, we create an easier path for them to follow the knowledge they have learned, as Proverbs 14:6 says: "Knowledge is easy to those who has understanding."

When our children develop an understanding of the Bible and its application to their lives, they also develop discernment and wisdom that follow them into all decisions in their lives, whether their parents are with them or not. We want to raise children who are spiritually independent of us and spiritually dependent on God and His Word. As they learn knowledge, they develop understanding; as they develop understanding, they develop discretion. As they develop discretion, they practice wisdom.

The best way to make application and answer the *why* of the Bible's stories is to ask questions. Let's follow this example of a story from the Bible that I taught my children when they were young. You could read this to your children and then follow up with specific questions afterwards.

Matthew 8:23–27: Jesus Calms the Storm (NCV)

Jesus got into a boat, and his followers went with him. A great storm arose on the lake so that waves covered the boat, but Jesus was sleeping. His followers went to him and woke him, saying, "Lord, save us! We will drown!" Jesus answered, "Why are you afraid? You don't have enough faith." Then Jesus got up and gave a command to the wind and the waves, and it became completely calm. The men were amazed and said, "What kind of man is this? Even the wind and the waves obey him!"

Questions to Ask that Engage the Mind and Heart

Mind How do you think the followers felt when they saw the storm rising and the waves covering the boat? (Afraid for their lives.)

Heart Have you ever been afraid in your life? When? Tell me the story.

Mind What was Jesus doing when the storm arose? (He was sleeping.) Why do you think Jesus could sleep in the midst of the storm? (Because He is God, and He controls everything; He wasn't afraid.)

Heart Do you think this was part of His plan to help His followers increase their faith in Him? (This question gives children a heart for the disciples.)

Mind What were the two things that Jesus said to His followers? ("Why are you afraid? You don't have enough faith.")

Mind What did Jesus show His followers? (He is powerful; the winds and sea obey him).

Heart Sometimes God allows difficulties to come our way so that we have an opportunity to have greater faith in Him. Did this increase the faith of Jesus' disciples? (Yes.)

Heart What did this miracle that Jesus performed teach you about His power? (He can do anything.)

Heart Let's go back to your story about a time when you were afraid. How can Jesus help you? How has He helped you when you were afraid?

Heart To solidify this passage in your child's mind and heart, which is a way for them to meditate, have them narrate this story in their own words.

Invite younger children (ages three to seven) to draw a picture of the story from the Bible on one side of the paper and then draw a picture of a time they were afraid on the other half. Ask them to tell you the story of both to you, a friend, their siblings, their grandparents, a neighbor, etc. Place the picture on their bedroom wall, and have them review it with you each evening before bedtime.

Invite older children (ages seven to eleven) to put themselves in the story by writing it out in their own words, using their own situation. For example, they might say,

> Jesus went to bed with me one night. A scary dream came to me while I was asleep with large monsters trying to attack me. Jesus was still sleeping. But I became afraid. I cried out to Jesus to help me. Jesus answered, "Why are you afraid? You don't have enough faith." Then Jesus woke up and gave a command to the bad dream, and it went away. I was amazed at what Jesus did for me. I realized that He was more than just my friend who is with me all the time. He is God, and even bad dreams obey Him.

You will notice that I used a simple version: New Century Version. Don't be afraid to use simple versions with younger children (three to eight years old). An effective parent will take what seems complicated and make it simple to understand. The goal here is to reach understanding in your child's heart, not to teach a grammar lesson or new vocabulary words. As they get older and their vocabularies grow, then transition them into more advanced translations like the NIV or NASB.

Many parents have used the Bible for academic instruction. Our forefathers did; this is certainly okay when used in the context of English lessons, but do not let that time be their only spiritual training. Let it stand for what it is: academic. Their spiritual training serves the purpose of heart change. We are training them for all eternity, not just this temporary world. I am not negating academics, but I am putting academic instruction in its proper secondary place.

As I mentioned at the very beginning of this chapter, the difference between the school of knowledge and the school of heart is that the former is of the flesh, and the latter is of the Spirit. One day, this flesh will be gone, but the soul lives on. We want to raise healthy, Spirit-filled children who will soar in their eternal states. Don't hold the secondary higher than the primary.

As we move our teaching from whetting with curiosity to piercing their hearts with application, we find that we need to sharpen our children's understanding of the Word of God by showing them how God's truth fits in the world they live in. This step is where children begin to see God all around them, not just in their home, family, and church.

To Sharpen Using the arts, literature, movies, and life situations to illustrate scriptural truth sharpens your children's belief. It is important to validate and solidify our children's knowledge and understanding of God's Word.

When I was in school, I thought that algebra was a waste of my time. I often thought, *How am I going to use this in my adult life?* Because of my lack of understanding, I saw this subject as something to get through, and I did not give proper value to the subject. Then I started to teach my own children. As I began to look at algebra again, I discovered that it taught children to solve problems. It taught them to be analytical and view challenges with the goal of finding solutions. While I never used equations in my adult life, I did develop a solution-oriented mindset that helped me to systematically solve all sorts of problems. Algebra suddenly had purpose, and I wanted my children to understand that its purpose was very important. The same is true with the study of God's Word. If we don't show our children how the Word of God affects their world, then we may (without intent) cause them to see it as an unnecessary component of life.

The way I show my children the value of Scripture in their lives is by helping them see it at work in their world. My husband and I did this through movies, literature, sports, and real-life situations.

When our children were young, my husband and I had a movie night with them once a week. On many occasions, we would parallel truths of Scripture with the movie watched. One in particular was *Beauty and the Beast.* While there are many parallels in this movie, the one that I pointed out to my children was the selfishness of the prince and how his selfishness caused him to be a beast in his heart. When we are selfish, we can be like a beast.

I explained that sin can cause us to be very selfish. However, the love of Christ frees us from this selfishness and helps transform us from being like a beast to being like Christ. Belle, the one who loved, gave of herself selflessly to the Beast. God gave of Himself selflessly by giving His Son to die for our sins. However, I explained that for His love to be perfect inside us and produce true change in our hearts, we need to accept His love and love Him back, just as the Beast accepted Belle's love and loved her back.

If you ask my children today if they remember this parallel, they would probably say they do not. But one thing they do know is the skill of applying God's truth in every aspect of their lives. Because we drew these parallels often from various movies, they naturally draw them out themselves today in the movies they see. They often will use movies to illustrate a point in Scripture when they teach others. They learned a skill, but they also learned to see Scripture as practical in their everyday lives.

My husband and I also used real-life situations (negative and positive) to show our children where God was working. A woman named Michelle at our church found out she had a brain tumor. She was a young mom with small children. It was devastating to hear this news. But this tragic time became an opportunity for the church to rally around her in prayer. This difficult time brought the people of God to their knees; when the surgery was scheduled, the church had a prayer sign-up so families could pray.

Our family signed up for an hour-long slot that day, and we continued this prayer time for a period of weeks. Our children were quite young at the time, but we prayed. They learned to pray for others. They learned that troubles do come into our lives, but God uses them to draw others to Him. Practically, our children understood Romans 8:28: "And we know that in all things God works for the good of those who love him, who have been called according to his purpose." Probably the most memorable statement my six-year-old daughter said was, "Mommy, I don't know Michelle, but praying for her makes me love her."

We see value in knowing the Lord ourselves and being committed to learning His Word so that we as parents are intimate with Him. Out of this relationship, we can impart God's truth to our children effectively. But this does not come without its challenges. Some children are hard to connect with. Some have strong wills; some have clashing personalities that conflict with their parents and their siblings. How do we reach these children? How do we get past these barriers so that we can foster a relationship that influences our children to love the

Lord? Our next chapter will dive into these challenges as we look at walking along the road in Deuteronomy 6:7.

Reflection and Review

1. Look back at Susanna Wesley's biographical sketch. What part of her life stands out to you? What areas of her walk with God or her view of relationships appeals to you? Why?
2. What is the value of storytelling with your children? Begin this process with your family, and share ways it strengthens the parent-child bond.
3. Explain what it means to whet, pierce, and sharpen your child's faith.
4. Pick a movie, and watch it with your family. Afterward, draw a parallel to Scripture with your children. Keep it simple. Share this experience.
5. Read Deuteronomy 4:9. What two instructions is God giving to parents in this passage? Why is following these instructions important?
6. Read Ephesians 6:4. How does just instructing our children in the knowledge of the Bible (without engaging the heart) provoke them to anger? What other dangers can form in our children's hearts when all we give them are rules to follow? What part of God do they miss?

Chapter Four

The Shepherding Parent

Unlike the false gods of this world, we serve a God
who seeks to be known and seeks to know.

I will never forget my fourth-grade English teacher, Mrs. Kelly. While
English is what I learned, relationship is what I experienced. Her willingness to teach and build confidence in me assisted my success. She
would sit with me, teach me, and patiently help me learn, no matter how
long it took. She would often talk to me about my family, my interests,
and my goals in life. She sought to know me. And getting to know *me*
at the beginning of the school year was not an easy task for a teacher.

Before attending this school, I attended the local public school
and, in essence, learned nothing. I am not against public school; this
school in particular did not do a good job of teaching the students in
attendance. The school was chaotic and the classes too large; because
I was not learning, I struggled with self-esteem.

My struggle in such a chaotic environment threw me into the
need to please people so I could feel good about myself. I wanted to
fit in and feel valued. I was a poor student, and when I showed up in
Mrs. Kelly's class, I was very behind. I couldn't even read! Yet Mrs.
Kelly saw potential in me; she took the challenge and went to work
in my life.

She began this task with one goal: to know me. Out of that knowledge, she began teaching. With each child in the classroom, her main goal was to build a relationship with that child, seek to understand him or her, and then disburse the information the child needed to learn. I soared in her class during the two years I was with her. The loss of education in the years before was made up in her class. While slow at first, I learned to read and write; I eventually picked up everything I lost and more. English became my best subject! Because she believed in me, encouraged me, appropriately pushed me, cared about me, and knew me, I rose above my inadequacies and experienced victory. The one reason I thrived in learning was because I knew that my teacher cared about *me!*

On the other hand, there was a nun who taught me in the later grades at this school. She was quite a character and was even asked to leave the school. Teaching may have been her gift, but relationship was not. She was hateful, discriminating, and jealous. Her condescending comments caused her class to do poorly. Most were afraid of her. Some made fun of her, and none had respect for her. I'm not sure there was anyone in *her* life who really knew *her*, and I definitely don't think anyone took the time to understand her. Later, I found out that she was mentally ill, and she was put in a hospital for help. I never learned how her situation turned out, but I do know that her behavior with her students distanced her from them and caused them to experience academic failure.

We serve a God who values relationship above all else. When asked by the teachers of the Law, "What was the most important commandment?" Jesus replied, "The most important one is this … Love the Lord your God with all your heart and with all your soul and with all your mind and with all your strength. The second is like this: Love your neighbor as yourself" (Mark 12:29–31). Relationship is at the core of Jesus' reply. Love directs our hearts to know *whom* we love. Out of that love, obedience flows, because we desire to bless the ones we are in relationship with.

We often see the word *neighbor* as the person next door, the poor we serve, the members of our church, our co-workers, and anyone who is *not* our family. In the Greek, *neighbor* means "friend." *Friend* indicates intimate involvement and close association. We often forget that our friends can be our children! We have intimate involvement and close association with each other. My children are my greatest friends. I know them, and they know me. When we look at Mark 12:31, we can see this more pointedly if we replace "neighbor" with children: "Love your children as yourself."

Too many parents see their relationships with their children as an employer-employee model: "I say; you do." Instead, we need to have a shepherd-sheep model; "I know you; you follow." While Jesus holds the office of the Good Shepherd, He has given parents the ministry of shepherding their children.

Only when we submit to Jesus' tutelage will we find victory in parenting. It's the only place we will raise children who are fully devoted followers of Jesus and who become influential blessings to our society. His example in knowing His sheep is our example as parents to know our children. In developing our shepherding ministry with our children, we have come to the second part of impressing God's Word on our children found in Deuteronomy 6:7: "When you walk along the road."

Relationship takes time, investment, successes and failures, rewinding and forwarding, patience, endurance, grace, and mercy. The questions posed are, "Where do we begin? How do we truly develop a relationship with our children that encourages shepherding?" Jesus paves the way to these answers as we look again at John 10:1–5 from a different angle:

Truly, truly, I say to you, he who does not enter by the door into the fold of the sheep, but climbs up some other way, he is a thief and a robber. But he who enters by the door is a shepherd of the sheep. To him the doorkeeper opens, and the sheep hear his voice, and he calls his own sheep by name and leads them out. When he puts forth all his own, he goes ahead of them, and the sheep follow him because they know his voice. A stranger they simply will not follow, but will flee from him, because they do not know the voice of strangers.

Know Their Name

My firstborn son, Matthew, is a strong-willed, sensitive, and loving son. He is unique in his ability to learn, as he learns best through relationship. The pathway to understanding for Matt is to reach his heart and foster his strengths through constant rapport. Teaching him at home was a challenge but also a joy.

In order for me to overcome obstacles in teaching Matt, I had to understand him. I needed to know *his name.* God does not deal with all His children in the same way. He is unique in His relationship with each of us. As parents following His example, we must do the same for our children.

When my son, Matt, was five years old, I began to truly study his personality. I read books on various personalities and the way children learned. I adjusted myself to his needs as a result. I have provided a reading recommendation list at the end of this chapter so that you can read and learn about these as you study your children.

It is important to know your children and understand how they learn and process life. Matt has a kinesthetic/auditory learning style. His personality type is phlegmatic/melancholic. His learning style means that he needs to move, be involved in the learning process, and hear the words being taught. He gained more when I read aloud to him; he comprehended more reading aloud himself. Books on CD were a plus and a need for Matt. Currently, he is in community college. He has discovered that being in the classroom and listening to the lectures profits him more than learning online. His personality dictates a great need for harmonious relationship.

Matt is gifted at teaching and is a great mediator in conflict. He has a deep need to help others who are hurting and struggling. He seeks truth and defends it. He has a sensitive side that needs recognition, and he necessitates talking through what he is learning and expressing his points with an apologetic view. He is strongly verbal in his processes. After reading and studying about him, I adjusted my teaching style to his needs. I found that he learned best when I sat with him and worked through the problems at hand, listened to him, and gave him an opportunity to discuss what he was learning. Doing this helped him grasp more and excel faster.

Matt thrives academically as a result of the relationship, not the knowledge studied. While teaching Matt took more time than my other three, I rejoice in the time, because he and I formed an incredibly close relationship that not only developed him academically, but also mentored his relationship with Christ. Truly, my time with him was a good example of walking along the road at its best!

This relationship with Matt has opened doors of influence in his adult life. He is twenty-two years old. He will move soon and will be transferring to a Christian University. While looking for a college for Matt, we determined it needed to be a college that offered a small environment, relational approach to teaching, and setting of empowerment so he could be involved in the process of learning. A larger university can instruct and disburse information well but can lack in the teacher-student relationship. People with Matt's personality and learning style usually get lost in the masses of a larger university and struggle academically. Knowing Matt's name has helped us choose wisely for him so he experiences success.

Knowing your child's name takes time; it requires learning what excites, motivates, encourages, builds up, and gives him or her worth. Knowing your child's name also considers what causes him to retreat, be angered, feel frustrated, and get discouraged. To effectively *know your child's name,* follow these actions:

1. *Read about personalities and learning styles.* Determine which one best fits your child. Learn the dos and the don'ts with these personalities and learning styles, and follow them. I learned to give Matthew space to process and organize internally; I recognized his gifts and pointed him to useful ways to use them. I also learned not to hurry or push him; if I did, I experienced his stubborn side quickly and ended up accomplishing nothing. I also discovered that his easygoing nature could cause him to become lazy; I needed to ward off this potential by keeping him focused on and accountable to his goal. This came with much talking and influencing him so he would not slip backward.

2. *Spend time in various situations with your children: at play, at school, at church, in social settings, on vacations, on field trips, etc.* Intentionally observe your children as they play and work with others, and learn how they receive and dispel information. Don't just observe, but also play and work *with* them. Listen to what matters to them. Don't dictate how they should play or work; instead, observe their actions. What do they talk about? How do they organize? How do (or don't)

they involve others? Use this information to determine how they learn and what their personalities are. Then use the information to point them where they need to be.

3. *Adjust yourself to their style of learning and to their personality.* We are the adults, and we can adjust ourselves. When children become teens and young adults, they can learn how to adjust themselves to others. But when they are young, it's hard for them to do this. They are still trying to grow into the little people God has created. Let them learn about themselves. Make a continuous "All About Me" book, and teach them who they are by how they learn and their likes, dislikes, motivations, strengths, and weaknesses. Strengthen their strengths, and give grace to their weaknesses. Have older children take personality, strength-finder, and spiritual gifts tests. Teens love to learn about themselves! After taking the tests, discuss their strengths and weaknesses so they can understand themselves and why they act and react the way they do. These tests give your children practical ways to utilize their strengths and gifts and work through their weaknesses.

4. *Never make them into little versions of yourself!* Too many parents try to relive their lives through their children. Allow your children to be all God created *them* to be. He did not give you children so you could have a second chance at life; He did not give you children so you could relive your back-in-the-day extracurricular successes. He gave you children so you could raise individuals who would uniquely serve Him with *their* lives according to *His* plan. It is not about us; it is all about Him and His plan for each person *He* created. We are all different, and our differences make His creation very good and beautiful.

Our passage from John 10 says, "He calls his own sheep by name and leads them out. When he has brought out all his own, he goes on ahead of them, and his sheep follow him because they know his voice." I have heard the old saying, "Kids don't care what you know until they know you care." This is very true. *After* Jesus knows the name of His sheep, He is able to lead them.

Lead Them

Children are natural seekers of approval. The approval they desire most is that of Mom and Dad. They innately want to make Mom and Dad happy; they want and need to know that their parents are proud of them. What child doesn't want her parents at her ball game, cheering her? What child doesn't want his parents watching his school play? Why do children even perform?

I know some children would rather their parents not come see them perform because of their fear of disappointing their parents. Some are afraid that they will fail simply because of the distraction that Mom and Dad are watching; they worry about what they are thinking instead of performing or playing. Either way, children seek to be known. Children are little people who have come into God's creation trying to figure out how they fit in. Their parents' approval (or lack of) communicates whether or not they are hitting the mark. If a child receives approval and develops a relationship with his or her parents, he or she is more likely to follow the parents' lead.

Most children are disobedient because they seek attention. The wrong attention from Mom and Dad usually encourages more disobedience, because sadly, wrong attention is better to a child than no attention. Wrong attention includes never seeing the good in their children, never celebrating their successes, only seeing their failures and pointing them out constantly, yelling at their child, demeaning the child's character with name-calling, ignoring the child with lack of discipline, and slack parenting.

Slack parenting is dismissing disobedience by blaming others for a child's behavior instead of trying to help the child take responsibility for his or her own actions and change them. Slack parenting also takes the form of pushing off parental responsibility on others instead of taking the role seriously. We see this often in school, where teachers spend more time disciplining their students than educating them, because the discipline is lacking at home. Finally, slack parenting can be considered loose, permissive, inattentive, and even idle.

Some parents make excuses for wrong behavior, or they simply bury their heads in the sand, not confronting the issue at all. They think that the behavior is a phase and hope it goes away only to find that a temper tantrum in a teenage body is uglier and less fixable than in a two-year-old body. The saddest part in all this wrong attention is children don't follow their parents' lead; they end up seeking others to follow. In some cases, they seek positive role models, like good teachers, coaches, and kids who are on the right path, but in most cases, they follow the wrong examples, get into more trouble, and acquire added ineffective attention. This is all they know.

In John 9, we find a great example of leaders who lead with selfish motives and wrong attention. Jesus healed a man who was born blind. After healing him, the man was brought to the Pharisees—the Jewish leaders of that day. The Pharisees only focused on the law; it was the Sabbath, and people were to do no work. Work included healing. They did not rejoice in this man's miracle. They did not notice that the man who was blind since birth was finally healed. The person's needs were of no significance to them; they only cared about their law. They were blinded by their lack of relationship with the man they were supposed to be shepherding. Additionally, they wanted to prove Jesus wrong and elevate their righteousness. Pride is a roadblock to spiritual insight.

In the end, this man didn't follow the Pharisees; he followed Jesus. He followed the one who not only healed him, but also pursued him. After being thrown out of the synagogue by the religious leaders, Jesus came to him at a desperate time. He cared for the man. He sought an individual relationship with the man that went far beyond healing his eyes. This man worshiped Jesus. In worship, we determine to follow Jesus' lead. We follow the one who *we know* will know us.

In John 9, notice the same wrong attention I mention that parents can give their children also being lived out by the Pharisees. We learn of the positive attention that Jesus modeled in this man's life. Following Jesus' example, we find that the positive attention includes the following:

1. *Seek to reveal God's glory in your children.* Instead of judging the blind man, Jesus compassionately saw opportunities for the glory of God to be revealed. "As Jesus went along, he saw a man blind from birth. His disciples asked Him, 'Rabbi, who sinned, this man or his parents, that he was born blind?' 'Neither this man nor his parents sinned,' said Jesus, 'but this happened so that the works of God might be displayed in him'" (John 9:1–3).

When looking at your children, don't see them through the lens of judgment or failure; see them through the opportunities of God. What can God do in your child's life? When you see failure in your child, seek God's power at work, for in the child's weakness, God is stronger.

Mrs. Kelly, my fourth-grade teacher, looked at me with potential; she saw beyond my failures and saw success. She aimed at the success instead of settling for my current state of lack. Because of this focus, I'm writing a book today!

2. *Seek to know the condition and needs of your children.* Jesus knew the blind man and his parents. He knew that it was not sin that caused the blindness, as in some miracles, sin was present. Jesus knew this family, and He worked to allow God's glory to be revealed.

"Jesus spit on the ground, made some mud with the saliva, and put it on the man's eyes. 'Go,' He told him, 'wash in the Pool of Siloam.' So the man went and washed, and came home seeing" (John 9:6–7).

Once you know your children, their needs, their personalities, and their learning styles, you can then begin to meet them where they are and lead them to God's glory. We can determine what is needed, as Jesus determined what this man needed. If it was forgiveness, Jesus would have forgiven sin, but in this case, the man needed to see, and Jesus made that happen.

What do your children need at this time in their lives? Do you know them well enough to supply what is crucial? Is it discipline, structure, encouragement, space, a nap, or some one-on-one time with Mom or Dad? It is good, right, and profitable for parents to pay attention to the condition of their children and give heed to their individual needs (Proverbs

27:23). This type of attention exemplifies being a good shepherd to your children, and it will increase their commitment to follow your lead.

3. *Believe in your children, see beyond their problems, and teach them to worship God.* In the end, the blind man did not follow the thieves and robbers (Pharisees). He followed Jesus; Jesus saw in whom God's glory could reside and shine. Jesus was able to look beyond the problem in the man and see God at work through him. The positive drew the man to his real leader. Jesus believed in the man, and the man knew it. The intimate love of Jesus pulled the man's heart to His. It was not wrath or condemnation that accomplished his change. Wrath and condemnation are the very elements that repel children from their parents. This is not much different from what the Pharisees did to the blind man.

"Jesus heard that the Pharisees had thrown the man out and when He found him, he said, 'Do you believe in the Son of Man?' 'Who is he, sir?' the man asked. 'Tell me so that I may believe in him.' Jesus said, 'You have now seen him; in fact, He is the one speaking with you.' Then the man said, 'Lord, I believe,' and he worshiped Him" (John 9:35–38).

The man's worship was an act of following the voice of His shepherd. "He calls his own sheep by name and leads them out" (John 10:3). Love your children into leading them. Leading means to know them first, tend to their specific needs, and draw them to your guidance with your love, not your judgment.

Going Ahead of Them

We serve a God who plans. He is a visionary. His greatest avenue of success is preparation and meticulous design. Jesus is a strategic planner who does not create out of whim. This is how He goes ahead of His sheep and prepares the path for them. Before He placed life on earth, He made sure earth could support life. Because of this character quality, we can trust Him as He goes ahead of us. Likewise, good parents research, plan, walk ahead of their children, walk alongside them, and lead them to pastures that satisfy, sustain, support, and send them forth with success.

How many children are left to figure out life alone today? For example, some parents make the decision not to instruct their children spiritually; they believe that their children should be exposed to all types of religions and make up their own minds. Some parents don't spend time with their children academically, leaving them to figure out lessons in isolation. This can be true in many cases when it comes to teaching children personal hygiene, sex education, proper relationships, how to be a good friend, character, etc. I can't help but put this poor parental leading into perspective through a few illustrations.

1. Would you take your child to a playground filled with broken glass and not tell him what to watch out for? Would you let him figure out his safety on his own?

2. You are at the farm, having a picnic. Your child drops food on the ground where horses have treaded and their manure has been dumped. Would you let your child eat the food anyway and let her figure out the right thing to do by experiencing sickness?

3. Would you allow your toddler to play with cleaning chemicals and learn the hard way that this is an unwise decision?

4. Would you allow your teenagers to wander the mall wit advising them of the dangers that loom in these places?

5. Would you send your young adult child on a mission trip without warning about good personal hygiene, the dos and don'ts of drinking water, and the dangers of sex trafficking, or would you just let her figure it out?

You would answer these questions with an emphatic *no!* Most of you would respond, "I would warn, instruct, and even in some cases keep these things away from my children."

It's important to realize that the spiritual decisions you make for your children when they are young will lead them to the right path or the wrong one. I say with the utmost of conviction that there is only one good path to take! That path is through Jesus Christ. There is no other name under heaven by which we will find eternal salvation! Letting our children just figure things out or choose from the plethora of religious options in our world is dangerous, even eternally lethal. Going ahead of your children takes place when parents follow Christ first, know His Word, and embrace His way of living. You can't give your children something you don't have.

There are many ways to go ahead of our children and prepare the way for them.

Going Ahead of Your Children Prayerfully and Prudently

Jesus was and is very connected to His Father. Likewise, our relationship with God needs to be as united. This type of prayer is intentional. Jesus worshiped His Father, and He also petitioned for His sheep.

Jesus' relationship with Peter is a very good example of parenting.

I love referring to them both. In the case of prayer, Jesus petitioned for Peter before Satan sifted him. Notice what Jesus said to Peter (Simon) when He foretold what would happen to him. "Simon, Simon, Satan has asked to sift you as wheat. But I have prayed for you, Simon, that your faith may not fail. And when you have turned back, strengthen your brothers" (Luke 22:21–32).

We discover two character qualities of Jesus in this passage that parents can acquire: prudence and prayer. Prudence means to be cautious. Jesus prudently warned Peter ahead of time that he was going to be sifted by Satan. Satan not only asked permission, but Jesus also knew Peter's ultimate response. Jesus knew Peter would struggle through this sifting; if Jesus had not known that, He would not have said that He had already prayed for him. Jesus also prayed for Peter. He prayed for his faith *before* the sifting took place. He prayed that Peter would not fail in his faith, and He encouraged Peter to use this sifting to strengthen others. He gave Peter warning, comfort, hope, and instruction. We see this in the following parts of the story:

1. Jesus warned Peter about Satan's sifting. Do we provide warning of the coming dangers—whether spiritual or practical—for our children?
2. Jesus comforted Peter with prayer. Do we pray for the upcoming trails our children will face so they are calmed with God's truth before the storm?
3. Jesus gave Peter hope that he would turn from this sifting. Do we give our children a view of God's hope in the difficult times of life?
4. Jesus instructed Peter to strengthen his brothers. Do we show our children tools for coping and overcoming the challenging

times they face? Do we give them a vision for God's purpose in times of testing?

Going ahead of our children requires four elements: warning, comfort, hope, and instruction.

Our children are being sifted by Satan every day. They face many temptations and struggles. They often become so overwhelmed by it all, they fall under it and are crushed. Without a prayer for them, they will fail! Sincere prayer is often the one thing parents don't take time to do for their children. They are good about instruction. Parents want to skip the first three elements and go right to the instructions, the lecture, the "what you need to do" part of going ahead of them. But without all four elements, we fail at helping our children overcome the sifting of Satan.

Parents need to commit to praying for children daily. How do we know what to pray for specifically? Through our intimate relationship with our children—by knowing their names—we can see the struggles they have by their facial expressions, body language, and conversations with us. I know when my children are struggling. I don't always know with what, but I can tell when something is wrong. At that moment, I begin to pray first that God will reveal the struggle to me so I can help them specifically and second that God will strengthen their faith and not let them falter under the difficulties they face. I pray for a way out, a way through, and a way up.

My son, Nick, is a good example of Peter. Not only does he often do before he thinks, but he also struggles verbally out loud. When Nick talks about something repeatedly with me, I know that he is in the midst of a struggle. Sometimes he does this with temptation, a decision he needs to make, or a problem he doesn't know how to solve. I listen, pray, ask questions, warn, and instruct.

Nick has usually already solved his problems at the point of me asking questions. He ends up discovering his own struggle, temptation, and solution. I credit this to my prayers for him more than my questions. In the midst of our discussions, I reveal to him where Satan is at work and where God can overcome. I share with him my prayers for him in his current situation. I encourage him that God can make a way of escape or a way through. Finally, I give him something to do. These four elements have effectively given me a foothold of influence with my children. Truly, influence's strength is in knowing my children and petitioning the Father for them.

Going Ahead Practically

Giving our children instruction is connected to understanding who *they* are and what works for *them*. Our instruction needs to aim for one mission: increasing their faith in God. Again, we come to Jesus and Peter. Peter knew fishing; it was his livelihood. It provided for him. Fishing provided a way to instruct Peter, reach him, and practically teach him new ways of faith.

In Matthew 17, Peter encountered tax collectors, who asked him a question: "Doesn't your teacher pay the temple tax?"

"Yes, he does," Peter replied. There is much to this story, but the focus for us is how Jesus used something familiar to Peter to give him new faith in God's provision. The Scriptures do not say how Peter felt or what he was thinking, but I bet he wondered how they were going to pay the temple tax. I'm sure they did not have the money, or Jesus would not have instructed Peter to go fishing, open the mouth of the first fish he caught, and find the four-drachma coin needed to pay their tax.

This miracle was for Peter specially, not for any other disciple.

Jesus intimately served Peter's need for increased faith. Jesus knew exactly what to use: fishing and money. Fishing *was* how Peter earned his living, and part of that living paid his taxes. However, Peter wasn't fishing anymore; he was following Jesus. In Matthew 4:18–20, Jesus called Simon (Peter) and his brother, Andrew. They were casting their nets—doing their jobs—and Jesus said, "Come, follow me, and I will send you out to fish for people." What did Simon Peter and his brother, Andrew, do? "At once they left their nets (their jobs) and followed Him." At this new point in life, Peter's provision came from total reliance on Jesus. This had to be scary and unsettling at times.

Our children face similar unsettling and scary leaps of faith in their walk with the Lord. How are we going to help them see Jesus at work so that their faith is increased? We can use the familiar in their life and show them something new about God.

By knowing your child's name, by knowing his or her struggles through intimate relationship, and through constant prayer with the Father, you can develop discernment about the needs of your child and the best ways to instruct him or her. Jesus knew what Peter struggled with before Peter even came into the house. Peter had not mentioned the conversation he had with the tax collector, but Jesus immediately referred to the situation at hand as He spoke to Peter. Jesus knew what He was going to use to help Peter increase his faith in God's provision. Jesus showed Peter that He was Lord over even Peter's method of livelihood.

Peter may have thought, *Well, if we have to pay the tax, I guess I could go fishing and earn the money needed. I could go back to Egypt, if you will.* Immediately, Jesus gave him clear instruction in how God provided for their need. What I love about this story is that Jesus took advantage of two things that increased Peter's faith and taught him a new way to see Jesus as Lord over all. We see the progression in this fashion: Peter feared for provision, Jesus used Peter's familiarity with fishing (an obstacle in his faith), and Peter learned that Jesus is Lord over all resources.

What things that are familiar to your children can you use to increase their faith? What matters to them? What reaches their hearts? Look to their passions and what they put their faith and dependence in. I have found that my children each have different needs, crutches, and challenges. I have used all these things to help them see that Jesus is Lord over them all.

Going Ahead Persistently

It's easy to become discouraged and deflated of all energy when it comes to parenting. We can succumb to the pressures of giving up and giving in. It's easier sometimes to just throw in the towel and claim, "I don't care anymore." How many preachers today would not be preaching if their parents truly gave up? How many men and women of God would not be men and women of God today if their parents threw in the towel? How many people's lives would not be transformed today if parents gave up on these children, who later became followers of Christ? Our decisions to quit affect lives that go unchanged in the absence of our endurance. It's not just our children who suffer from our feebleness to keep on going, but also all the people that God will change through them. Where would the church be today if Jesus gave up on His disciples?

Jesus endured constant bouts of deficient faith in his followers. He dealt with pride and sinful hearts in each of them. Jesus taught, tested, warned, exposed, encouraged, prayed, and never gave up. He did this all the way to the cross; He even forgave all when He hung on the cross in the most detestable, mortifying, painful experience any human has ever endured.

It is totally horrifying to know that those whom you invested all of your time and energy in for three years deserted, betrayed, and denied you during one of life's most difficult times. When Jesus needed His followers the most, they scattered, not to be seen anywhere while Jesus was spit on, flogged, dragged, and sadistically and shamefully killed before all the people whom He taught, healed, and loved. Yet in all this, He found it in His hurting heart to forgive, and He beseeched His Father to do the same. He cried out to heaven, "Father, forgive them, for they do not know what they are doing" (Luke 23:34).

As parents, we need to remember the faithfulness of Jesus when our children fail again and again. When Jesus carried His cross to His death, He didn't look at the spit, the insults, His pain, or His heartache from rejection. He looked at the result of His sacrifice—the eternal healing each could experience. His focus was on the payment for sin, the finished product—the end to the curse once and for all.

When your child is in the clutches of sin or the bondage of failure, look to the perseverance of Christ to gain your endurance. Look to the finished product of God's grace. Focus on the goal ahead and not the journey getting there. Aim for the glory of God in your child.

I grew up without a father; I had minimal if any interaction with him. But I had a mom who possessed the endurance of Christ. She went ahead of me with persistence. I struggled with self-esteem. I was a people-pleaser, and it was not all due to poor academic learning in my early years. It also stemmed from not having a father in my life who showed me love. As a result, I sought love in all the wrong places.

From ages of twelve to sixteen, I dabbled in drinking, graduating to drugs. I hung out with the wrong crowd and got in trouble continuously at school. I tried to overcome this lifestyle. I sought help at church in the youth group. My mom prayed for me and taught me the right path to take. She put me in Awana, youth group, and church; she spent time with me, loved me, and encouraged me. However, I was stubborn, and the more I engaged with the wrong people, the more I became calloused to any form of authority, discipline or wisdom. Nonetheless, there was a small part of my heart that wanted what was right and pure.

There was an inkling of hope in my soul. I know my mom saw it, and that was the part she aimed to draw out of me. There were times when this hope surfaced, and I tried to get on the right track; then the thorns of life crept up and choked that hope right out. This went on for a few years until my mom boldly placed me in a rehab. I was stubborn and strong-willed, and it was fourteen months before I came home.

My story is intense and would encompass a book in itself, but the point I make is that my mother never gave up. God used her persistence in praying, encouraging, and rallying around me to show me that He was there and loved me no matter what. I would not be where I am today if she had not been this kind of parent.

I met a girl in rehab who knew Jesus. She loved Him with everything. This rehab facility was not Christian; as a matter of fact, it was evil and criminal. In this very dark place, God planted this amazing young girl to help me trust fully in Jesus and not people. She taught me much in the short time she was there about reading the Bible, understanding its truth, and how to implement it in my life. She made Jesus incredibly real to me, and for the first time, I knew what it meant to make Him Lord of my life and the father I never had.

The funny thing about this whole experience is that this girl was there for a brief time. I believe that she was placed there for the sole purpose of bringing me to Jesus, because once I committed my life to Him, she was gone. I have yet to find her. She is a result of my mother, grandmother, and a group of parents going ahead of me in persistent prayer. I have often wondered if she was an angel in human form sent to me who was to inherit salvation; I have thought this especially after recently reading Hebrews 1:14: "Are not all angels ministering spirits sent to serve those who will inherit salvation?" It makes sense that she very well may have been an angel, as Hebrews 13:2 also says, "Don't forget to show hospitality to strangers, for some ... have entertained angels without realizing it!" I have no idea who she was, but I do know that she was there as a result of persistent prayer on my mom's part.

As long as your child has breath, there is always hope for his or her salvation. Your persistence will not only go ahead of your child, but could also be the very quality that saves him or her! Never give up; too much is at stake. When you want to throw in the towel, send up prayers instead. When you want to give in, press in to the Lord. When you want to give up, give hope and encouragement to your child.

We are in a battle for the souls of our children. Battles are not won when soldiers give up; they are won through sacrifice, courage, tenacity, and determination. When fear seems to loom larger than the courage to press forward, remember the words of Swiss theologian Karl Barth: "Courage is fear that has said its prayers!" The same is true when it comes to apathy, exhaustion, and hopelessness. Put all that energy into prayer, and then watch the salvation of the Lord take place.

71

Reflection and Review

1. What does "knowing your child's name" mean, and what are ways to accomplish this?
2. Describe your child's personality, learning style, and gifts, and list ways you can adjust yourself to them in order to accomplish reaching God's design for his or her life.
3. Read John 9, and list ways the Pharisees gave wrong attention to the blind man. List ways Christ gave the right attention.
4. In what ways do you think you give wrong attention to your child? In what ways do you give the right attention? What are the three things that parents can do to encourage their children to follow their lead?
5. What does it mean to go ahead of your children? Describe the three ways we can go ahead of our children and how you can implement these in your parenting.
6. Why are the four elements of warning, comfort, hope, and instruction important to give to our children?
7. Some great books to read that will help you study your child's learning style, personality types, and spiritual gifts are *The Way They Learn* by Cynthia Ulrich Tobias, *Teaching with Heart: A Guide to Cherishing and Challenging Children in the Christian Classroom* by Jody Capehart, and *Discover Your Child's Gifts* by Don and Katie Fortune. Choose one of these books to read over the coming months. As you read, study your child. Discover your child's learning style, personality type, and gifting. Begin to adjust yourself to your child's God-given design.

Wide in Influence

Chapter Five

The Suffering Parent

We all know people who have been made much meaner
and more irritable and more intolerable to live with
by suffering: it is not right to say that all suffering
perfects. It only perfects one type of person—the
one who accepts the call of God in Christ Jesus.
—Oswald Chambers

Often when life seems difficult, we find that the Spirit of God will lead us into the wilderness instead of the land of milk and honey. You would think that when we are in an oppressed state, God would take pity on us and relieve us from our suffering. But He chooses the wilderness. He chooses the way of holiness.

It feels like the aim of the wilderness is to strategically submerge us into more disdain. "Why, Lord?" we cry out. All we want is an escape route. Because God is in total control, He sometimes uses the very things that are oppressive and isolating to liberate us. The very wilderness He places us in takes our lack of faith and turns it into total reliance on Him. We learn to have a holy submission to God's will. And what likens a dusty desert becomes our beautiful place of refuge.

We never know what arduous times are held out for our lives or for our children. We do know that in this world, we *will* have troubles; we *will* experience the wilderness. Jesus promises us this in John 16:33: "In this world you will have trouble. But take heart! I have overcome the world." Often we forgo the latter part of this passage; all we can see is the trouble. We forget that Jesus has overcome the world (and all its challenges); we overlook the meaning of "taking heart," which is being totally reliant upon the promises of God.

Parenting is filled with mountains and valleys. The mountains make us feel triumphant; they can give us feelings of success, peace, and confidence. But they can also puff us up, causing us to be judgmental and even self-righteous. This is where the valleys of life give us an ever-needed wilderness experience. In the wilderness, God humbles, disciplines, and poises us for grace and ministry to the hurting and hopeless. In the wilderness, God prepares us and our children to be wide in influence.

My family has experienced many wildernesses and humbling situations. We all remember when God called me to leave my position as a part-time children's minister to accept a full-time position at a church in our community. Just before this, God called us to move to a small town fairly far away from familiar friends. As a result, my family had to change churches. My husband even left his good-paying, full-time, ten-hour-a-day position that included a two- to three-hour commute in order to partner with me in this ministry. In doing this, we both took a step of faith; he quit his job to help with the kids and the ministry and to look for a supplemental full-time job in the community where we lived.

We knew that his position would mean less pay for the same amount of effort and work on his part. However, we were obedient to God's call, regardless of the financial lack it brought. We moved, we changed churches, I took the position, and my husband found a job. At first, it seemed that we were doing okay with the decisio made. However, behind the scenes, these changes caused anxiety and depression in our daughter. This became the catalyst to a Spirit-led wilderness.

The Path to Influence

When Ashleigh was very young, she was often afraid of the dark. We used to sing Psalm 56:3–4 by Steve Green: "When I am afraid, I will trust in you. In God, whose word I praise." We ended up memorizing all of Psalm 56:3–5. For a long time, this was her favorite passage. She often came into our room in the middle of the night, afraid. I would get up, take her back to her bed, and lie down with her, and we would sing this passage until we drifted off to sleep. This gave Ashleigh great comfort when she was afraid; it also taught her to use the Word of God as a tool to encourage herself in life when difficulties arose.

Ashleigh's childhood consisted of wonder, laughter, reading, and cooking. She was always a giving person; she had friends whom she shared Jesus with. She loved dance, sewing, and art. Going to the farm, riding her bike, going to the park, taking long walks, and swimming in the creek were all joys she cherished in her childhood. I'm grateful that her favorite part of each day was our Bible lessons.

Ashleigh's aunt asked her once, "What's your favorite subject in home school?" Her reply was, "Bible." And it was. She loved to hear and read the stories of the Bible. At age three and a half, she began reading. This did not happen because I taught her; she watched me teach her older brother, and she taught herself. Of course, I continued that teaching, giving her tools to further equip her. She had a deep need to read so she could satisfy her curiosity. Her love for the Bible would eventually be what saved her and gave her purpose through a testing time of life.

Ashleigh has always been curious, serious, mature, bright, and a bit of a melancholic child. She has always had a rare sensitivity to the hurting—so much so that her understanding of others' pain was realized by feeling it herself. However, because she was young, this desire and very sensitive gift from God overwhelmed her and spun her into a deep depression between the ages of twelve and fourteen. This happened just about the time my husband and I were called to make life changes in our family's residence and our vocations. These changes in life coupled with her deep need to help the hurting raised questions for her, and she desperately needed to bring clarity and purpose to her life and her vulnerable and delicate gift of mercy.

When Ashleigh was twelve, my husband and I noticed a difference in her personality. She became very quiet, reclusive, and segregated from the family. She often wanted to be locked up in her room alone. I was concerned about this. I asked her how she was, and she always said, "Fine." But as a mom, I knew things were not fine. I prayed often, and I sought creative ways to find out what was wrong. I had a few close friends praying for her too.

I have always prayed a specific prayer for each of my children:

> Lord, if our children are in sin, I pray they are caught so we can right them on the correct path. Lord, if our children are having difficulties of some kind, I pray You make this known to us so we can help them through their struggle. Lord, keep us appraised to what our children are into, and make us ready to handle whatever it is with Your grace and Your truth.

I can honestly say that God has been faithful to that prayer with each of our children. I often prayed this for Ashleigh during this trying period.

The time came when God acted on this prayer. I received a phone call from a mom of Ashleigh's friend. The mom was concerned because of an e-mail Ashleigh sent to her daughter. The e-mail indicated that Ashleigh was depressed to the point of possible suicide. You can only imagine how my heart sank and the horror I felt over what could have been if this mom had not had the courage to call me. I will always be grateful to her!

This resulted in an intentional approach to Ashleigh's healing. During this situation, I struggled with a lot of doubt in my parenting. I wondered, *What have I done to cause this?* I often cried out to the Lord and asked Him to show me where I messed up. I wanted to fix my problem. I felt like a failure, and often my own heart dove into despair. But I will never forget the impression God laid upon my heart one day when I sought Him in tears.

It was as if He said aloud to me, "This difficulty is not because of something you have done or not done. Just like I have loved you enough to walk *you* through the valleys of life to teach you to rely on Me, I also love Ashleigh the same, and I am walking her through her own wilderness so she will know Me deeply. This depression is *for* Ashleigh, not against her."

This word from the Lord gave me a whole new perspective on parenting. No longer did I believe the prideful lie that if a parent does *A,* then the child will reach *B.* No, God does not work that way, for "In *her* heart *a mom* plans *her* course, but the LORD determines *her* steps" (Proverbs 16:9, emphasis added).

Just before this wilderness, I figured I knew all about parenting. Thus far, parenting was pretty easy for me—exhausting at times, but fairly smooth in all. Because of this, I thought I had arrived. I was rightfully humbled and learned to rely on God's ways, not my own.

At the beginning of this difficult spell of Ashleigh's life, my daughter did not talk to me about her feelings or what was going on inside her. It seemed hard for her to articulate the emotional pain she felt.

In the middle of one night, I was awakened by the Spirit of God and prompted by Him to go into her room and gather her journals. Ashleigh loves to write, and I knew if I read her journals, I would find out what hurt my little girl's heart. This act may seem like an intrusion of her privacy. It was, but I like what a counselor said to both of us: "Your privacy is a privilege; however, when that privilege is violated and harm to yourself or others comes into play, the privilege must be taken so help can be given." Therefore, I acted on this good advice and the prompting of the Spirit of God. I read the very thick stack of journals; it took me four hours to read through them.

My tears were great. My heart ached for my daughter, but my soul praised God all the same. I learned what questions she had about herself, what struggles she encountered with her faith, and the pain she experienced because of many changes in her life. I discovered her desire to help others, her hurt, and her confusion.

In addition to this, I was moved to praise God. Ashleigh's journals were filled with pages of Scriptures she had learned over the years along with heartfelt prayers written in the form of cries to her God. This truly brought me to my knees. In the midst of this, an impression came from the Lord again: "You have taught her well; you have led her to My Word, and it is this that will heal her. Now your mission is to walk with your daughter, get her the help she needs, and counsel her through this dark time of her life so she can see My light."

After two years of counseling, medication, and spending a great deal of time with Ashleigh, she found healing. She found answers to her questions about life, and together we "continued to work out *our* salvation with fear and trembling" (Philippians, 2:12 emphasis added).

Great benefits came from this struggle. Ashleigh and I went from being mother and daughter to sisters in Christ. Ashleigh learned to rely on the Lord in ways she never knew she could; she felt His love in a way that caused her to dance with joy and freedom. She was able to put all her energy into helping other girls work out their depression and hopelessness through the Word of God and helping them find their identity in Christ. She has developed into an incredible woman of God whose faith is strong and unbreakable. Her sensitivity to the hurting has enabled her to forge ahead in God's calling. Even though these times were difficult for her, she learned to use the Word powerfully as she wrestled with her faith and found purpose in her suffering. In the end, she discovered a ministry of influence from her pain.

At the conclusion of this dark time in her life, Ashleigh and I both felt God's call for her to go on a mission trip. This trip was the conclusion of this wilderness for her and the entrance into the promised land of milk and honey. She decided to use her gift of dance and join the dance team of YWAM (Youth with a Mission) in Montana and eventually went to Germany. Her healing from depression is best described in a blog post she wrote while on this trip on June 22, 2009:

On the Road to Freedom

The theme of my summer so far has been freedom. When I left home, everything I read in the Bible or anything I read or heard was about being bound and free. I thought that God was just calling me to free the brokenhearted and captives (Isaiah 61:1–3). But he had even better plans. He wanted to free *me.*

The details aren't really important, but what *is* important is that as I spent my time here (in Montana) with God, he revealed to me the many things that were holding me back from him. Sometimes God asks us to do hard things, and sometimes that hard thing is to let go of the things that you think you can't live without. God is amazing when you let him dig out the pain in your heart and soul and make you let go of it so that you can experience *peace* and *freedom.*

I wasn't going to share this, but I feel compelled. I love how *free YWAM is* in their worship … in pretty much everything. These people live by the Holy Spirit, and it's truly amazing. They've shown me how much of a real person God is. Anyway, during one worship time, there were people standing, singing, not singing, raising their hands (or not), sitting, lying face-down, kneeling, crying, smiling, and dancing. They just responded to how God moved, and this one time, he moved me out of my comfort zone. He wanted me to dance. Although I've always loved the song "I Won't Relent," I finally got what it meant. Out of nowhere, I saw how God had always pursued me throughout my whole testimony. God was *there.* And *he* pulled me through. It *was God who wanted me here in this place to experience all of this and all of his love. Before I could let myself deny him, I kneeled down and took off my shoes. Then I started to dance, and the Holy Spirit moved through me, and I wasn't even in control of how I moved anymore. God was dancing with and through me. It was similar to adrenaline but a little different. I never got tired. All the faults that I have when I dance in class were perfected, and even though I danced with my eyes closed, I never once ran into a wall or a person. Letting God move you is true freedom. When I was done dancing, all I could do was weep, because in that moment, I knew the three things that I had been asking God: I knew that he was really there, I knew how much he loved me, and I knew that I was free.*

I will never forget the impact this blog post had on me, where I was when I read it, or how I felt. My love for my daughter (as well as my boys) is deep and strong. My prayer and hope have always been that they love the Lord with all their hearts, souls, minds, and strength. When they struggle, I struggle. When they hurt, I hurt. When they feel joy, I feel joy. God has given me a bottomless longing to see my children wrapped in the arms of their heavenly Father.

When I read this blog post, I was a leader at a Christian camp with my boys. One of my friends had access to the blog on his phone and showed it to me. I was standing outside in the middle of the courtyard of the campus where we were staying. I read the blog post, and my world came to a halt. My tears flowed with joy, and my heart was lifted in praise to our great God. My daughter was free! And she taught me something—"to live my life every day in the movement of the Spirit of God." I needed this truth in my life at that moment, and I have never forgotten it.

I had two choices when this trial came into my life. I could praise God in the storm and be blessed, or I could grumble through the storm and be depressed. I chose the former and have been fortunate to experience a deeper view of God than I had before.

When we are faithful to give our children Jesus and His Word, when we walk with our children in their struggles, when we patiently wait upon the Lord to bring them through, we can count on the promise that God will break forth like the dawn. Our healing will quickly appear, our righteousness will go before us, and the glory of the Lord will be at our rear as a testimony of His faithfulness to us. We will know with certainty that when we call, the Lord will answer; when we cry to Him for help, He will say, "Here am I" (Isaiah 58:8–9a).

In the dessert, our cries go from "Why, Lord?" to "Yes, Lord!" With holy, tenacious reverence and complete peace, we will say with assurance, "I will choose to learn, not fail. I will choose to trust, not doubt. I will choose to obey, not defy. I will choose to praise, not whine."

The Israelites wandered into the desert after being freed from Egypt's oppression only to be more oppressed by their own sin in this barren, unnerving place. However, God's test was their liberty. But they chose to fail; they chose to doubt, defy, and whine. They chose to die in their sinful state.

Jesus, on the other hand, was led in the desert; He was hungry and tempted by the Devil, but He won. He won because He chose faith, not food. He chose docility, not defiance. He chose worship, not wailing.

If we are willing, in our wilderness, we can find freedom and peace. In this very desolate, unwelcoming station in life, we find God's open arms without distraction. We discover God's person in ways that were never known before. His reality becomes our truth. His ways become our habits. His wilderness becomes our victory. Our misery becomes our ministry!

I am here to testify that our misery becomes our ministry. I have written this book as a result of many ups and downs in parenting. I hope to encourage the parents who walk with God but find themselves in the valleys and need lifting. I challenge parents who do not walk with God to walk with Him so they can give their children Christ. I wish to motivate parents who have the desire to walk with God and give Christ to their children even though their parenting marks no implementation to move on that desire.

Choosing to prevail in the midst of the current dust of our lives is not easy. It's hard! It's draining. It can sap us of all energy. Can you imagine how the Israelites felt after wandering in the desert for forty years? We judge them, but in all honesty, I understand their failings. It requires much commitment and perseverance to believe God in these debilitating times. But in these wilderness experiences, God equips us. We move from being deep in Jesus to being wide in influence. Yes, the Israelites failed in this situation, but there are other accounts in the Bible where people prevailed under circumstances that were just as hard—and we can, too!

Moving from the Wilderness to Influence

Elijah is a good example of this. He lived in a time of overwhelming evil. Ahab was King of Israel, and he did more to arouse the anger of the Lord than all the kings of his nation. With fierce boldness and reliance upon the Lord, Elijah went to King Ahab and proclaimed the Word of God: "As the Lord, the God of Israel, lives, whom I serve, there will be neither dew nor rain in the next few years except at My word" (1 Kings 17:1).

Elijah announced this to King Ahab, fully understanding that he would also be affected by this judgment. Therefore, God sent Elijah to the wilderness—the Kerith Ravine. Here, Elijah learned total dependence upon God's provision. That is what a wilderness does for us—teaches us total dependence on God's provision. Elijah had nothing to fall on but God. On the one hand, King Ahab (the king who could order his murder) hated him. On the other hand, the curse God put upon King Ahab and the nation of Israel robbed Elijah of his own needs. Elijah found himself in a time of learning.

In obedience, Elijah went to the ravine and waited for God's provision. God provided him with water from the brook and ravens who served him bread and meat in the morning and evening. God is faithful to servants whose hearts are willing and obedient to His purposes. In this time of learning and growing deeply in his relationship with God, Elijah was prepared to influence another who lived in her own wilderness: a widow in Zarephath.

Sometime later the brook dried up because there had been no rain in the land. Then the word of the LORD came to him: "Go at once to Zarephath of Sidon and stay there. I have commanded a widow in that place to supply you with food." So he went to Zarephath.

When he came to the town gate, a widow was there gathering sticks. He called to her and asked, "Would you bring me a little water in a jar so I may have a drink?" As she was going to get it, he called, "And bring me, please, a piece of bread."

"As surely as the LORD your God lives," she replied, "I don't have any bread—only a handful of flour in a jar and a little oil in a jug. I am gathering a few sticks to take home and make a meal for myself and my son that we may eat it—and die."

Elijah said to her, "Don't be afraid. Go home and do as you have said. But first make a small cake of bread for me from what you have and bring it to me, and then make something for yourself and your son. For this is what the LORD, the God of Israel, says: 'The jar of flour will not be used up and the jug of oil will not run dry until the day the LORD gives rain on the land.'"

She went away and did as Elijah had told her. So there was food every day for Elijah and for the woman and her family. For the jar of flour was not used up and the jug of oil did not run dry, in keeping with the word of the LORD spoken by Elijah. (1 Kings 17:7–16)

A way through the wilderness is understood in this passage of Scripture. There is an escape that helps us retain the lessons learned. We see the steps taken by Elijah, and then we see the same steps taken by the widow.

Elijah *obeyed* God when God told him to go to the Kerith Ravine. He *waited* for God's provision with faith and trust. Elijah *accepted* God's provision without complaining, only learning, and he was *equipped* to go and teach God's faithfulness to a widow, who walked in her own wilderness.

The widow *obeyed* Elijah's instructions to fix him a piece of bread first. She *waited* for God's provision, as He had promised through Elijah. The widow *accepted* the provision God had given

Elijah, her son, and herself, and she was *equipped* for the next wilderness in her son's life.

Obeying, waiting, accepting, and equipping are all a part of growing through the wilderness of parenting. Obedience to God's Word in raising our children, waiting on our prayers to be answered, waiting for our children to respond in faith, and accepting the trials and troubles of life with hearts of learning equip us for the next wilderness and the next person who needs our testimony.

In 1 Kings 17:17–24, we see a change in the widow. She went from obedience to faith as a result of Elijah's influence on her.

Sometime later, the woman's son became sick. He grew worse and worse, and finally he died. She then said to Elijah, "O man of God, what have you done to me? Have you come here to punish my sins by killing my son?"

But Elijah replied, "Give me your son." And he took the boy's body from her, carried him up to the upper room, where he lived, and laid the body on his bed. Then Elijah cried out to the LORD,

"O LORD my God, why have you brought tragedy on this widow who has opened her home to me, causing her son to die?"

And he stretched himself out over the child three times and cried out to the LORD, "O LORD my God, please let this child's life return to him."

The LORD heard Elijah's prayer, and the life of the child returned, and he came back to life! Then Elijah brought him down from the upper room and gave him to his mother.

"Look, your son is alive!" he said.

Then the woman told Elijah, "Now I know for sure that

you are a man of God, and that the LORD truly speaks through you." (NLT)

Let's answer Elijah's question: "O Lord, my God, why have you brought tragedy on this widow who has opened her home to me, causing her son to die?" It was for the purpose of taking this widow from obedience and knowledge of God to faith in His truth.

This is exactly what our wilderness produces for us: complete reliance on the Lord. We don't know the influence these wilderness encounters had on this widow's son, as Scripture does not point this out. But what this widow gained cannot be contained. She most likely led her son to God as a result of her own faith. She modeled for him the same steps she walked: obeying, waiting, accepting, and equipping.

From a very young age, Ashleigh knew who God was, and she even knew His Word well. But it wasn't until she walked through the wilderness of depression that she made God her God, not just her parents' God.

Ashleigh did not discover her faith randomly in her wilderness. There were intentional approaches and acts on the part of her parents. An intentional act on the part of Elijah helped this widow believe the truth of God. Our influence upon our children is as important as the resources we hand them. Just sending them to church is not enough. Telling them to read their Bible on their own is not enough. They need mentoring, teaching, and dialogue with their parents. They need relationship!

The wisdom of Proverbs tells us clearly that a parent is to "guide their children in the way of wisdom and lead them along straight paths" (Proverbs 7:11). The key words in this verse are *guide* and *lead*. To guide is to point out and show, and to lead is to march in front of the one following; these meanings indicate a hands-on approach to parenting. Our job is not just directive but inclusive.

Every month, I create a Bible reading plan for the children in my children's ministry to use as a reading guide with their parents. A few weeks ago, on Sunday morning, I was filling in for one of my volunteer teachers in the second and third grade classroom. It happened to be the first Sunday of the month, and I encouraged each child to take the Bible reading plan home and follow it with his or her parents. Then a sad thing was said by one of the children: "I don't have time to read the Bible."

Another child piped up and said, "After I go to school all day and go to soccer practice, I'm too tired to read the Bible."

Many were in agreement with these comments. My heart ached for these children. You see, these children will one day be teenagers, and they will experience a wilderness. Will they be prepared? Will they experience victory? Will they have the success of Jesus and Elijah in the wilderness, or will they experience the failure of the Israelites? Parents, teach your children the Bible. Give them success for eternity! They need Jesus! If anything warps this plan in your life, take it away. Whatever keeps you from reading the Bible with your children is not worth keeping, especially if it means watching your children struggle in the wilderness and fail.

When Ashleigh's depression hit my family, it would have been easy and even understandable to be depressed and despair. No one would have blamed me for being down, but God could not have used me in that state. When we choose to be down, our state becomes a great seeding ground for Satan to rob, steal, and destroy us. I had to intentionally seek what God was doing in this trial. I had to obey into feeling. I had to seek the good coming from it. We are promised that "in all things God works for the good of those who love him, who have been called according to his purpose" (Romans 8:28). I hung on to that promise; with great zeal, I prayed for God's goodness to be revealed in the midst of the wilderness.

I am asked when I share this story, "What did you learn from this time in your life?" People want to know, "How did you come out on top?" They don't want to know how I plumbed the depths of despair and gave up. What inspiration is in that? How does giving up help others? How does losing heart glorify God? The biggest thing I learned from this time in my life was to walk with my children through their valley and give them hope in Jesus. Initially, when Ashleigh was depressed, I wanted her to heal very quickly, but that was not God's plan.

Walking with my daughter took compassion, listening to her, affirming her feelings, and understanding her instead of seeking to be understood by her. I learned to be patient with her healing, I studied her and acquired ways to encourage her. I chose not to judge, push, or freak out on her, but instead to empathize, tread slowly, and pray. Being her friend and sister in the Lord became very important to me. I grew even more than I can put on paper. I became my daughter's mentor and coach. This far outweighs being just her mom. Would I go back and change this time in my life? Never! I rejoice in the fruit this difficulty brought; I have learned to do my best work as a parent on this uphill bit. At the time, I did not even know my best was being polished.

In hindsight, I learned to embrace God's promises. I know now that the things that happened to me have actually served to advance the gospel in my daughter and many in her life today. The best way to view the wilderness is to seek good in the midst of the challenge. Change the question from "Why, Lord, why do I have to go through this?" to "What good is God doing; what ministry is being birthed?"

Reflection and Review

1. What wilderness experience have you faced or are you facing right now?
2. Read Matthew 4:1–11, and write the ways Jesus was successful in His wilderness experience.
3. What lessons can you implement in your life as you read about the wilderness experiences of Elijah and the widow?
4. What is the most important step you can take in your children's spiritual lives today? How will this step prepare them for the future wilderness encounters that await them?

Chapter Six

The Serving Parent

The best way to find yourself is to lose
yourself in the service of others.
—Mahatma Gandhi

Amy Carmichael is one of my favorite missionaries. She took obedience to God to a courageous level. She was marked with qualities
of leadership, compassion, and service that should be imitated by
all of us, *especially parents.* She was responsible for saving young
girls from prostitution in the Hindu temples located in India. She
founded the Dahnavur Fellowship, a place she made home for these
abandoned children.

Amy's goal for the children she ministered to was to help them
become good soldiers of the Lord Jesus Christ. She knew that good
soldiers serve; they are not interested in being served. They wish to
please their commanding officer. She took seriously following the
footsteps of her commanding officer, Jesus: "To serve, and to give
his life as a ransom for many" (Mark 10:45).

She influenced the children she rescued with this same paradigm.
She was not just interested in rescuing the children, but also restor-
ing them. A served person is a rescued person, but a serving person
is a restored person. These children were abandoned, humiliated,

demoralized, and corrupted. Each one who came out of this life had to feel useless and unworthy of anything important. Amy wanted to do more than snatch them from the fire. She wanted them to find purpose from the flames.

The Dahnavur Fellowship was a home that valued training, productivity, and service. Once children arrived, they were cared for, educated, and made a part of the family. Each had a part in serving the whole. Each learned a skill. Each submitted to one another with grace, mercy, and hard work. Amy did more than give hope to these children; she gave them a future. Once these children grew to be adults, they served new children who arrived; these children in turn served yet new members of the family. Today, this great place Amy began in 1901 still thrives.

Because service to God was in Amy's heart, she was not interested in a comfortable life but a contributing life. She loved God so much that her heart wanted to worship Him and learn from Him as He moved her to give of herself to others.

Let's rewind a bit and answer the questions, "What made Amy a servant instead of a consumer? How do we raise children today who have servant hearts like hers?"

It was common practice for Amy's family to meet the needs of the impoverished in their community, even if this was frowned upon by the elite of their society. Most people of her day walked by with snubbed noses when they came across the homeless, the lame, and the filthy. But the Carmichael family helped, ministered to, and did what they could to ease the hardships of the downcast.

Along with her siblings, Amy was brought up to view her things as opportunities to share with others. The Carmichael children did not see themselves as elevated above another but on an equal plane. Her family gave her vision for the eternal versus the temporary; the parenting style of Amy's parents challenged me to be the same with my own children.

Amy's parents truly stand out as examples, for if her parents were not driven to please the Lord and fulfill His will, then Amy would not have been the one to rescue the many children in India who were doomed for evil. Amy's parents played a huge role in her future endeavors. They may not have gone to India with Amy in person, but they surely did in character and training. Likewise, parents have the same significant role in their own children's lives if they choose to take it seriously.

Reading the biography *Amy Carmichael* by Kathleen White reveals that Amy Carmichael's heart to love and serve the Lord also caused her great suffering. She experienced all sorts of needs. She faced danger and endured great illness and pain. Yet regardless of the difficulties, she kept this paradigm: "Life's not a level or smooth road; but it is a blessing to scale the hills and trudge over the stones with a good heart." She felt that "one does [his or her] best work on the uphill bits, though one may not know it."[6]

From Amy's positive view of difficulties, she learned much, helped deeply, and founded a ministry that still prospers today. Even after her death, she still speaks.

Amy's upbringing was the stepping stone that propelled her to affect many in India. Amy's parents took to heart the practice of Deuteronomy 6:4–9 and created a home filled with God's glory and grace for their children. God's aim is to build a home that clearly marks His presence from heaven to earth, from earth to our homes, from our homes to our hearts, from our hearts to our children, and from our children back to the world. It's a cycle of God's constant power flowing upon, within, and around us. This practice is consistent with Deuteronomy 6:8–9: "Tie them as symbols on your hands and bind them on your foreheads. Write them on the doorframes of your houses and on your gates."

God has a bigger plan for our children then just being taught at home and being raised to love God. His plan reaches far beyond the four walls of the interior. His intentions are to take our children to the ends of the earth and make a permanent impact on the lives of the people within their influence. Essentially, our responsibility as parents is to raise them deep in Jesus so they can be wide in influence. Besides teaching our children the word of God, it takes two intentional actions to help them be an influence on others: parents willing to serve their children and empower them to serve others.

Amy's childhood consisted of sharing with her siblings, which caused her to feel the need to serve the sick and the poor. Living for the eternal, she elevated God's sovereignty above her temporary comforts. She trusted God's provisions and she valued balance between fun and work. Fulfillment, rather than filling a need, was a priority for her when training children. She believed that life's satisfaction came from knowing God, growing in His grace and truth, and loving people with a heart like His. Her parents did an amazing job at imparting the mind of Christ and the heart of His will to their children.

Parents Who Serve Their Children

We live in a consumer-driven, me-focused world. We see this often in families, and sadly, we see it more in our churches than we should. People even choose and/or remain in churches based on what they receive, not what they can give. With this mindset, parents unintentionally teach their children to view serving as a contingency upon what they receive from others instead of what God has given.

I have found that serving is probably more essential to my own spiritual growth than attending services. I have also discovered that service sanctifies our children's faith. Without it, they falter; with it, they flourish.

When my husband and I first moved to the town we currently live in, we visited many churches, trying to find one that God was calling us to be a part. This took months of searching. One Sunday, we sat in a church service, and Matthew, our son said, "It really feels strange to just sit in church and not be doing something here." I smiled and knew that we needed to find a church soon, for my children's hearts were burning to give, and I didn't want to lose that.

Since my children were very young, service has been a huge part of their lives. Where did my children begin this mindset of serving others? With my husband and I and with their siblings. If parents model service to their children and if children learn to serve their siblings, they can get along with anyone. This is not an easy behavior to live or train in our homes, but I can confirm that nothing is impossible with God.

I like what John C. Maxwell says about leadership: "You've got to love your people more than your position."[7] Parents have to love their children more than their positions. Service starts with us. Jesus, our Savior and leader, came to serve. Likewise, parents were given to their children to serve them, not just to teach them to serve. Again, you can't give your children something you don't have or do yourself.

Philippians 2:1–5 gives us very clear principles that guide us into true servanthood; while this passage is for all people, we will look at it in respect to parents and their children.

Is there any encouragement from belonging to Christ? Any

comfort from his love? Any fellowship together in the Spirit? Are your hearts tender and sympathetic? Then make me truly happy by agreeing wholeheartedly with each other, loving one another, and working together with one heart and purpose. Don't be selfish; don't live to make a good impression on others. Be humble, thinking of others as better than yourself. Don't think only about your own affairs, but be interested in others, too, and what they are doing. Your attitude should be the same that Christ Jesus had. (NLT)

This passage starts out with questions. Every question needs an answer; yet in this passage, every question gives us a way to serve our children. The first one speaks of *encouragement.* Have you experienced encouragement? You know what that feels like, and you certainly know what it feels like to not have the encouragement needed. The first way to serve our children is to verbally encourage them. Share with them how you are proud of them, and specifically tell them areas in which they are doing well. Children are starved for positive reinforcement, and encouragement often dispels many discipline problems. It's amazing how an encouraging word can change a child's course of action.

Our second question speaks of *comfort.* Children today face an awful lot of sin. They face heartache from hateful words spoken to them by their peers; they encounter disappointments in school, sports, and other activities. Encouragement often relates to a job well done, while comfort gives hope when life is hard and failure hits. Comfort them with listening ears and responses like "I understand" or "I can relate." Point them to the hope Jesus' power can give them to try again and keep on going.

Our third question broaches the subject of *fellowship with the*

Spirit. We know that the Spirit of God lives in God's people. When I think of fellowship with the Spirit, I think of time with my Christian friends. My children are greatly encouraged and comforted when they can spend time with friends. Friends are a big deal to my children. This becomes even more crucial when they are teenagers. They develop their own identities as they hang out with friends, and this builds confidence. Fun and work should be balanced, as Amy Carmichael believed; children should make time for their community.

Our home is the teenage hangout. Our children have always looked forward to having their friends over and simply enjoy hang time. The fridge is open for all; we pull out the games, watch a movie, simply talk around the table, and just have some good old fun.

One day, I drove one of the boys hanging at our house to church for band practice, and he said to me, "I love hanging out at the Cramseys'." I asked him why. "Because you and Dan spend time just talking with everyone."

Does taking time for our children to have fellowship with friends require work on my part? Have we had to repair a few holes in the wall? You bet! But the rewards are great. The reasons I enjoy having my children's friends at our house are that I know where my kids are, I know who their friends are, and my husband and I can have an influence on those who come to visit. It's a win-win, in my opinion. There are times when my kids' friends will show up on clean the house day, and guess what? They clean! You can't beat that!

Our fourth question speaks to being *tender* and *sympathetic*. Both these actions are crucial when it comes to serving our children. To be *tender* means to be affectionate, kind, warm, and gentle. Affection is one thing that I think gets most neglected today by parents. There is something about a hug, a kiss, and a touch that seems to get lost as the kids get older. The human touch is healing, especially when life is stressful. Our children (young or older) need our touch. Hug them, rub their backs, give them a pat on the shoulder, and give them a kiss goodnight or hello.

Our boys are very affectionate. I'm grateful that when they reached their teen years, they still gave their mom and dad hugs. I have not experienced them not wanting to be seen with us in public or not wanting to hug us. Our daughter is not so affectionate and has never been. But that has not stopped us from giving her a hug when she needed one or rubbing her back on a stressful day. Our children need affection; it assures them they are loved and accepted.

A *sympathetic* parent seeks to understand and not just be understood. Parents can be so busy, they forget that they need to stop and listen to their children when they share their day or their struggles. It is also tempting to lecture our children and insist that they get what we are saying without hearing them through. It doesn't hurt to allow them to have a different point of view and explain it. We don't have to agree. Being considerate and sensitive to their opinions opens doors to further communication. They will feel supported, and they might be more agreeable to our point of view if we give them the floor.

We move from questions in this passage to instructions: *agreement, love,* and *working together.* All three of these require give and take on the part of parent and children. But the parents are the lead. What is modeled by the parents will be imitated by the children. These three instructions are followed by a goal: *to achieve one heart and one purpose.*

There have been many times when my children don't agree with my instructions. One in particular is whether to allow them to obtain their driver's license at the age of sixteen or nineteen. The more my husband and I read through their driver's training manual for their online classes, the more we were convinced that cognitive and responsive maturity in handling a vehicle was not on their side at age sixteen. We concluded that this was not the case just for our children, but for all children at this age. We wanted them to have as much practice in all situations as possible before taking on such a dangerous responsibility. Therefore, we decided that they could get their permit at sixteen and then their driver's license at nineteen. For the most part, we didn't get a lot of rift until our third son, Nick; he wanted his driver's license at seventeen.

Nick is my most verbal child and wanted to argue this point with my husband and I. We decided to listen and consider his request. He is a very responsible son and wants to please and obey us, so we weren't worried about his reasons behind driving. My husband and I prayed and considered his points, but we still stuck to our decision to wait until he was nineteen.

My son came around, even though he didn't agree; he came around because he trusted his father and me, we listened to him, and he knew that we had his best interest at heart. In the end, we came to an agreement out of love and working together. Our goal was oneness of heart and mind. We would not have had this privilege of unity without a good relationship with our son.

We move from questions and instructions to now the don'ts. Don't be selfish; don't live to make a good impression on others. Don't think only about your own affairs. All three of these reek with pride if not obeyed. This is where a selfish focus plays a huge role in our culture. I think the best way to see the value of these don'ts is to see their negative fruit if not obeyed in our parenting relationship.

When parents take the stand of "it's all about me," they leave their children feeling neglected and oppressed. Don't be fooled in thinking that your kids don't know when you are about yourself and not them.

They may not know the *why* behind the behavior, but they do know they stand second fiddle in your priorities.

Selfish, people-pleasing, and self-absorbed lives cripple relationships. These character flaws distance parents from their children. As they become more distant and this goes on, it becomes harder—even impossible—to gain the relationship back. And guess what? If you lose the relationship, you lose your influence in their lives! Someone else will get it. And that could be a bad thing or a good thing, depending on who your kids choose to impact their lives.

The antidote to these three flaws is also included in the passage from Philippians. Be humble; think of others better than yourself, and be interested in others and what they are doing. Proverbs 11:2 says that "with humility comes wisdom." And Proverbs 11:25 reveals that "he who refreshes others will himself be refreshed." Being interested in others and what they are doing is a reflection of true, godly love. It is not rude and certainly not self-seeking (1 Corinthians 13:5).

When I think of the word *refresh,* I think of being recharged. When I recharge my children, they in turn recharge me. The bond we create from selflessness enlivens the friendship, so our effect is stronger and lasting.

I can certainly attest to being very busy. Being a wife, mother, minister, home school teacher, homemaker, friend, and daughter gives me many roles to fill. Each has its time commitments. A good friend told me when my oldest was three years old, "You don't have to stop your roles to be a good mom; you just have to be willing to be interrupted." It was good advice. When one of my children needs to talk and I'm working, cleaning, or cooking, I can be stopped; I can listen and give them my full attention. I can be stopped for my friends and others I minister to. Being interruptible keeps people first and tasks and things second.

Too many parents are consumed with their own affairs. They don't have time or are unwilling to stop and take an interest in their children's lives. This is not only selfish, but also damaging to the personhood of their children. We see this lived out at ball games when dads or moms are on the phones instead of watching their children play their game or when children are talking at home and mom and dad are far away in their thoughts. Another scenario is the literal absence of Mom and Dad.

I like the antidotes to these behaviors. The opposite of selfishness is humility, and humility brings wisdom. Wisdom is more than knowledge and truth; it's perception, good judgment, and insight. When we choose to humble ourselves to serve our children, we glean a true perception of where our children are in life; we are able to be compassionate and use good judgment in the decisions we make for them. Finally, we are able to glean insights about our children that help us grow closer to them in relationship. Your relationships with your children will give you the best leverage for influence in their lives forever! When they move out and move on in their lives and when you pass on from this life, you will still speak to your children!

It's really simple. Put the phone away. Ask specific questions so you can pay attention to your children. Attend their extra-curricular activities, or better yet, get involved! Be there! Time is short; before you know it, they will graduate from high school and then from college, get married, and possibly move hours away from home. Your time is now. There isn't a tomorrow for your children; it's today. Take it or lose it.

It might be easy to be immobilized by regret over past failures with your children, but don't let that keep you from moving forward. I like what Mother Teresa says: "Yesterday is gone. Tomorrow has not yet come. We have only today. Let us begin."

I am not saying that your children can interrupt you without respect or without waiting for you. Teaching them proper channels to interrupt you that show you respect and gives you a chance to separate from an activity is certainly reasonable. I have noticed over the years, though, that because I am interruptible, my children will take the initiative to wait for me to finish something and then speak to me. If for some reason I'm not able to be interrupted—which is seldom but happens—they trust that I will get to them when the first chance arises, because it has been their experience. Children trust past behaviors, not good intentions.

Ultimately, if we are going to serve our children with servant hearts, we need to develop the attitude of Jesus Christ. The only way I know to have the mind of Christ is to saturate myself with His Word. The more I know who Jesus is and how He handled situations, the more I will imitate His ways. It always comes back to His Word.

The heart of this matter is that we all want our children to be blessings to others in society. We want them to be remembered by their giving hearts and utilized with their God-given gifts. Philippians 2:1–5 is our guide. We should be able to implement the value of serving in our children if we model it for them first.

I like the quote about service by Gandhi: "The best way to find yourself is to lose yourself in the service of others." The key phrase in his quote is "lose yourself." Jesus said something similar: "If anyone would come after me, he must deny himself and take up his cross and follow me" (Matthew 16:24). The way to follow Jesus is be a servant, not a lord. The only way I know to really lose my self-centeredness is to look outside myself and meet the needs of others.

God doesn't just mean for us to only serve the homeless, hurting, and underprivileged. Our children need our service just as badly. I know of parents who will go and serve everyone else while leaving their children uncared for. They are known for their incredible hospitality and compassion for others, while their children go the way of the world. These parents don't realize that their children will one day be the needy being served later in life because of their parents' neglect. Keep your children a priority, and serve the needy in your community *with* them, not instead of them.

Creating servant hearts in our children starts with the parents, but helping our children serve others starts with tangible opportunities we give them. In the next chapter, we will look at practical ways that help children be the hands and feet of Jesus so they can influence their world.

Reflection and Review

1. Read Philippians 2:1–4. What ways of serving our children are indicated in this passage?
2. What areas of serving your children according to this passage stand out to you? Why?
3. Where do you feel affirmed in your service to your children? Where do you feel challenged? What are your next steps to meet that challenge?
4. Why is relationship our best leverage of influence in parenting our children?
5. As it relates to serving our children, what does the quote by Gandhi, "The best way to find yourself is to lose yourself in the service of others," look like?

Chapter Seven

The Empowering Parent

You may never know what results come of your action,
but if you do nothing there will be no result.
—Mahatma Gandhi

Two years ago, my children and I were running errands. On our way
to have lunch at Chick-fil-a, we saw a young man who was homeless standing on the grassy island in the middle of the highway.
Immediately, my son, Scott, said, "We should bring him some food
from Chick-fil-a." We all agreed that it was a good idea. We ate our
lunch and then ordered his food. We all put our money together and
bought him a meal, a drink, and a milkshake. We were excited! Off
we went to give this man his lunch.

He was standing on the island that separated a very busy highway.
I could not park the car, so I drove and let my children out so they
could meet the guy and give him his lunch. They gave the man his
lunch and spent time talking to him; then they circled around him,
laid hands on him, and prayed for him. I sat in the car watching with
tears running down my face. I was amazed by their love for this man.
This man's name was T. J., and since then, they have prayed for him.
We may never know the impact they had on this person, but we do
know they had an impact still.

The interesting thing about this incident was that the meal was *their* idea, not mine. They led the way, not me. I simply facilitated their desire to serve this man. On their part, this took leadership, risk, and courage, not just service. If it were just service, it would have been my idea, and they would have obeyed what I asked them to do. Instead, they looked with eyes wide open for opportunities; once the opportunity presented itself, they responded with their own planning and implementation.

I could have said *no.* I could have stifled their desire and eventually hardened future attempts to serve. I had to die to myself and my agenda to allow them to spontaneously give of themselves to another. Was I busy that day? Yes, I was. Did we have time? Not really, but somehow, God worked it out. I was the one blessed to see my children lead and minister to someone who was hurting. "He who refreshes others will himself be refreshed" (Proverbs 11:25).

My children and I did not know why this man was homeless; knowing the reason why was irrelevant. All we knew was that the Holy Spirit prompted us to move, and all we had time for was to follow His leading. I like what Mother Teresa said: "If you judge people, you have not time to love them." Service is about loving people. All we can do is give; God will take care of the rest.

The best way to teach our children to serve is to inspire, permit, and release. These all define empowerment. Empowerment does far more than action. If we just teach our children to act but do not empower them to lead, we limit their God-given abilities to effect growth in others. They may influence, but they need to produce growth. The kingdom of God thrives on growth, not just influence. Influence is the catalyst to growth. Growth is contagious; it spreads and causes more people to move forward in His will.

Inspire Them

Inspiring our children takes getting involved with people who hurt. This is important, because in order for children to be effective at serving others, their hearts need to be impacted by the other person's situation. The next step is to have the courage to feel another's pain. There are many ways to accomplish this at different age levels.

When our children were much younger, they developed a heart for others by first developing one for each other. They learned to serve their siblings; they were taught to open their eyes to see each other as people who feel. My husband and I encouraged them to listen to each other and take turns talking so that all could hear each person. They affirmed one another and cheered each other at their ball games or recitals. We urged them to teach each other skills or assist with chores. When one hurt, we taught them to pray for the one in pain. They created a genuine concern for each other.

Today, my children are very close. The bond of love between siblings is deep; if children are given time when they are young to cultivate this bond, they will always remain close. Parents have to spearhead this. Trust me—it won't happen naturally. I see too many siblings who have no concern for each other. They amplify hatred and chaos in the home. This can be a strain in the family and the marriage between Mom and Dad.

I like what Amy Carmichael's parents taught their children. "From infancy, the Carmichael children were taught to share their possessions, and no class distinction was ever observed in the Carmichael home."[8] This was true in my home, too. My children were required to share their belongings with each other and to share with their friends. My husband and I taught them that people were more important than things.

Another way my husband and I gave our children a heart for the hurting was through books and movies. We read books to our children that helped them feel for others—biographies of missionaries, *Old Yeller, The Little Princess,* and *The Ugly Duckling,* to name a few. You can get a better idea of which books to choose for your family by ordering *Books Children Love: A Guide to the Best Children's Literature* by Elizabeth Wilson. I used this often to select good, wholesome books for my children.

Choose books that are age-appropriate; there is no need to introduce disturbing situations to your children before they are ready. Even Jesus was cautious at what He shared with his disciples, for He told them, "I have many more things to say to you, but you cannot bear them now" (John 16:12 NASB). Jesus was sensitive to what His followers were able to take in. We must parent our children with the same consideration.

My husband and I also taught our children to pray for specific people who were hurting in our family, the lost in our neighborhood, our church, and friends. We visited people and delivered meals to them. As our children got older, we served food at the homeless shelter; they participated in service projects with their youth group and went on mission trips. At church, every Sunday, they use their God-given gifts serving on a ministry team that interests them. We want them to see that others need their help and that their lives are not their own; their lives belong to Jesus. Service is at the heart of who Jesus is and we want our children to develop Jesus' mind and character.

These types of things cause our children to see their world outside themselves. They give purpose behind the service. If we don't know why we are serving or know the positive effects service has on people, then we aren't very motivated to do anything. Service at that point just looks like grunt work, not God work.

Permit Them

Parents initially steer their children toward opportunities of service. But in time, if serving is a way of life for a family, children are going to have ideas of their own. It's important to allow them to take risks (with guidance) and create their own ways to serve others.

Recently, our son, Nick had an idea to start a soccer ministry in the park. It was more of a pick-up soccer game for anyone who wanted to join in. His idea was to engage with the kids who hung out at the park but were going nowhere in life. Most of them don't know Jesus. After offering a pick-up game, he wanted to read a few verses from the Bible to anyone who wanted to stay and listen. He started this ministry a few months ago, and unfortunately, it rained the first day it began. He was disappointed. My husband and I supported him and told him to not give up but to try again. We gave him hope that God would bless his efforts in time. Sometimes our children's ideas are not going to work at first. This is where we need to revisit their vision and encourage them.

My daughter and her friend wanted to create and perform a dance musical for a family service at our church. Because I was the leader of this ministry, I had the opportunity to allow her to use her gifts of choreography and dance along with her friend's gifts of directing to make this happen. Using their gifts coupled with my Bible knowledge and writing, we developed an amazing production called "Journey to the Earth." The storyline was about Jesus' journey from heaven to earth seen through the prophecies and promises that started in the Old Testament and realized in the arms of Mary. It was amazing! Many people saw it and were blessed. The beautiful thing was that it built confidence in my daughter and her friend to continue to use their gifts for the Lord.

When we give our children opportunities to lead, we permit them to make service opportunities their own and give them momentum to advance on to bigger possibilities. They grow in their faith and ministry through this empowerment.

Our children will fail at times, and we never want to underestimate the lessons learned from these failures. These failures are good; the flops of life teach and grow them. The goal is not perfection in our children; it's reflection of our Savior.

Release Them

One day, your children are going to get to a point where releasing them is the next step of independence. My daughter and I had an amazing ministry together at our last church. After her depression, God used this time in our life to create a ministry from this trial. I found myself counseling young teenage girls and their parents through similar problems. However, counseling the girls was not enough. Like my daughter, they needed discipleship and relationships within the body of Christ in order to completely heal and grow.

In the meantime, while I counseled the girls, God called my daughter to lead a small group of high school girls through the Bible and help them grow spiritually. She came to me with this idea, and I was excited. I couldn't do any more at the church, and this was a great opportunity for her to give to others and grow in her own leadership. So it was decided.

Ashleigh and I met for leadership coaching weekly, and she led the group of girls every Tuesday afternoon. This group grew from three to eighteen over a very short period of time. Our approach to the ministry included me offering family counseling to the girls and their parents and Ashleigh inviting the girls to her group. This continued for two years. These girls got a holistic approach to spiritual growth.

My daughter eventually became a leadership coach to other teenage girls so they could lead groups. This ministry grew, and God changed lives!

Empowerment involves many phases for our children. At first, they shadow us, watching us serve others. Then they serve with us, accepting a little more responsibility each step of the way. Finally, they are able to lead on their own with mentoring from time to time. We then find them serving and empowering others. Service and empowerment are gifts we can give our children. They feel useful, not used. They feel wanted, not weary. They feel hopeful, not hassled.

The great men and women of God were givers, not takers. They did impossible things for the Lord and the people He loved. Likewise, this gift of service ushers our children into the position of the same great cloud of witnesses. They reach a point where they influence others rather than just being the influenced. They become the arrows in the hands of a warrior that Psalm 127:4 speaks about.

A Deeper Service

Empowering our children to lead and serve is a good goal. We would never want this to be our only goal, though. If we did, we'd be no different than a nonprofit organization that serves the poor but never restores them to Jesus. We want our children to "really know Christ and experience His mighty power that raised him from the dead … and learn what it means to suffer with him" (Philippians 3:10).

Let us focus on the phrase "suffer with him." What made Jesus suffer on the cross? Where was His real pain? Ezekiel 33:10 tells us His heart: "I take no pleasure in the death of wicked people. I only want them to turn from their wicked ways so they can live." God's real pain is seeing the people He loves choosing to live apart from Him and die eternally without Him. This needs to be our pain, too. We need to share in this suffering with Jesus so that we will do something about it. Let's face it; whether it is physical or emotional pain, we do what we need to stop it. If we truly are pained by the lost and dying all around us, we will arrange our lives to meet the goal of bringing salvation to their lives.

Heavenly honor is earned by sacrifice, giving of oneself for another, and becoming like the lowly. Mother Teresa was this type of person. She chose to live with the poor so she could minister to the poor. She chose to become poor so she could understand their station in life. Mother Teresa truly grasped what it meant to share the sufferings of Christ. Her suffering was so deep that she literally felt the pain Jesus felt for the lost. This pain escorted her into what she called "the dark night of her soul."

This is the epitome of service we need to desire and live. This is the highway of holiness we need to get our children to. Mother Teresa's prayer was to never refuse anything that God gave her to do; she also desired to have the suffering heart of Jesus. She was captivated by His love at a young age and wanted desperately for the hurting in Calcutta to know His love and embrace it like she had. I think she wept when she saw the suffering in India, just like Jesus wept for Jerusalem. These tears of sorrow can only be obtained through a saturation of hurting people in our lives.

The best way our children can be true servants is to drink the cup of sorrow that Jesus spoke of. I don't necessarily mean the cup of martyrdom. Our children should love people enough that nothing else matters but telling others about His love for them. Giving our children a heart for the lost makes them servants above all servants.

I have children who hurt for the lost. I particularly have two who have been neighborhood evangelists. The last neighborhood we lived in was one of the most profitable places to live for the kingdom of God. We lived in a cul-de-sac, and this neighborhood was truly a mission field! I could tell you countless stories of times when my children shared the Lord with their friends and how many in this cul-de-sac were changed and effected by the gospel of Christ.

After the terrorist attacks of September 11, 2001, it was suggested that people stockpile duct tape, water, and extra food for emergencies. My children were young, and I was homeschooling them that day. It was a crazy day. I had lots of interruptions: the phone rang, and people were at the door. It seemed the school day took an eternity to get through. I was incredibly frustrated. By the afternoon, I finally had one more subject to cover with my two older children before dinner needed to be prepared.

The day before, I had decided to share with my kids about the possible attacks that our country was expecting, and I wanted to give them hope. So I shared with them the weapons we have as Christians that can help us through any attack: the armor of God from Ephesians 6:10–18. I had no idea that this would come in handy the following day.

I worked with Matt and Ashleigh on their last school lesson for the day when the doorbell rang. Frustrated, I mumbled all the way to the door, "Not another interruption." It was Ashleigh's friend, Lindsay. She was a sweet, bubbly girl who spent a lot of time with us that year. But when she walked into our house, I could tell something was wrong. Fear marked her face.

I welcomed her into the school room so I could finish Matt and Ashleigh's last science lesson. While teaching them, I couldn't stop noticing how unhappy Lindsay was and how fearful she looked. I submitted to the Spirit's promptings, we put away the science lesson, and I asked her what was wrong.

Lindsay shared her fear of the terrorist attacks and of dying. She worried that all of her family was going to die, too. She was visibly terrified. Immediately, God brought to my mind the armor of God. She did not come from a Christian home; however, my family had prayed for her for a while and had at many times shared Christ with her. I could see this was a real opportunity to give her eternal hope.

I told Lindsay that she could have powerful weapons to fight the terrorists. Her eyes lit up. Matt and Ashleigh immediately knew what I was talking about, as we had just covered this the day before. I started to explain each weapon from Ephesians 6, and then Matthew and Ashleigh took over the explanations, describing each one with illustrations that Lindsey could understand. In all the excitement of explaining the weapons, Matthew piped up, "And if we die, it doesn't matter, because we're all going to a better place anyway!" Well, that last statement didn't exactly make her feel better. However, we knew that God was definitely at work in this room!

I asked Lindsay if she had ever asked Jesus to be her Savior. She said she prayed every night, but nothing seemed to happen. I explained sin—that it separated us from God's love but that God loved us enough to send Jesus to die for our sin so that we could be forgiven and He could live inside us through His Spirit forever. Then I asked her if she wanted to use one of the weapons. Her face brightened, and with an emphatic *yes,* we chose prayer, the last weapon in the passage. We all held hands and prayed with her to receive the Lord as her Savior. This was far more important than any science lesson!

We never finished the science lesson that day, but we finished a lesson on bringing someone to Christ. This would carry my children into their future so they could truly serve Christ by fulfilling His deepest desire: bringing the lost into His family.

I love the lyrics to the song "Hosanna" by Hillsong United. "Break my heart for what breaks Yours; Everything I am for Your kingdom's cause." We need to pray with our children just like Mother Teresa and ask God to break our hearts for what breaks His. We need to aim our lives at one purpose—bringing people to Jesus for God's kingdom cause. Nothing else should matter!

Essentially, our lives are no different than those of Noah and his family. They boarded the ark and heard all their friends outside the ark drowning and dying. All around us, people are drowning in their sin; they are dying. When we don't tell them about Jesus, it's as if we bought them a ticket straight to hell.

I need to be more attentive in this area than I have been lately. It is very easy to get lost in our Christian circles and forget our purpose here on earth.

I find that when my life is busy, I forget to feel the things God feels. I run and run, and my life misses the heartbeat of God. When we do so, our children follow suit. It's good in those times to go away, spend time in prayer, and ask God to give us back His heart. Better yet, we should ask God to help us give our hearts back to Him. He is the potter, and we are the clay. We can ask Him to create pure hearts and renew steadfast spirits within us so we will teach transgressors His ways and so that sinners will turn back to Him (Psalm 51:10, 13).

Powered by God's Spirit

Paul's heart for the church and the lost was balanced. He cared deeply for the ones who followed his teachings, and he cared deeply for the ones who did not know the Lord. His ministry life was filled with work, travel, tragedies, and difficulties; yet he still had a heart for those far from God. His reliance was not on himself, though.

Paul instructed the Colossian church with powerful words about his mission here on earth and where he got his energy. We can certainly take it to heart and make it ours. "He (Jesus) is the one we proclaim, admonishing and teaching everyone with all wisdom, so that we may present everyone fully mature in Christ. To this end I strenuously contend with all the energy Christ so powerfully works in me" (Colossians 1:28–29).

It takes all the energy of Christ to have a heart like His. Our hearts must be completely yielded to His work in us. I thank God that His power is available to us and our children. We do not do this alone. We can't. We cannot reach the lost, serve the poor, submit to one another, and be the servant leaders Jesus calls us to be by our might or power; we can only be these "by God's Spirit" (Zechariah 4:6).

With Paul as our example, we can't complain about our busy schedules. If we are too busy to serve others and reach the lost, then our schedules need clearing. I say this as much to myself as I do to you. If we want to effect eternal change in the lives of people around us, we must be willing to change things in our lives to make this a reality.

I recently learned how to shoot a gun. This is my husband's and my new fun activity! We love going to the shooting range. I'm not a good shot, but I'm not bad, either. There is something invigorating about shooting a gun. We went to a shooting range near our home, and every time I shot my gun, I was all over my target. My husband discovered that the target was too far away from me. There was just too much distance for me to overcome in order to hit the bull's eye. He brought the target closer so I could see it more clearly and have more impact. *Boom.* I hit the bull's eye!

Reaching people who are lost is much the same. The closer we get to them relationally, the more influence we have on them. The closer we get to our own children, the weightier our influence on them. Getting closer to people and our children will mean removing the distance that distracts so we can fulfill our life's aim. You have to ultimately figure out what that distraction is in your life. If you remove those distractions, you, your children, and the kingdom of God will be more fruitful!

Reflection and Review

1. The difference between being a servant and being empowered is the difference between the law and Jesus. The law effected coercion; Jesus effects conversion. Keeping this in mind, in what ways do you empower your children to serve? Where do you need to improve?

2. What is the benefit of raising empowered children instead of raising serving children?

3. According to Colossians 1:28–30, what should be our primary purpose in life this side of heaven? Where do we gain our energy to accomplish this purpose?

4. What testimonies or illustrations in this chapter stood out to you? Why?

5. Empowering our children has a process: inspire, permit and release. Describe this process and how you can implement this with your children in a specific serving opportunity.

Chapter Eight

The Sending Parent

And how can they preach unless they are sent?
As it is written, "How beautiful are the
feet of those who bring good news!"
—Romans 10:15

I shared in a previous chapter about my daughter's depression and the freedom she found in Christ, especially when she went to YWAM in Montana. But I did not share my experience of sending her on mission. This is a critical piece to parenting, because our role as parents to our children is to not keep them but send them. Oh, how I would love it if it were to keep them! Rightly so, this is not God's plan. How can those without Christ know Him if we don't send those who do know Him? (See Romans 10:15.) We want to raise children with beautiful feet, not just feet.

There were many forms that needed to be filled out to approve Ashleigh for the YWAM mission in Montana and ultimately Germany. As my husband and I filled the forms out, we came across one on which her parents were to give YWAM permission for her burial or transportation of her body in case her life was ended as a result of the mission. You can only imagine my thoughts! Before signing, I wanted to say to Ashleigh, "No! God's not calling you to this mission!" However, I knew that those thoughts were not God's; they were mine. I was an overly worried mom who loved her daughter very much.

In the end, I knew my resistance to letting her go was due to my lack of faith in God's provision for her. Additionally, I was convicted by God's Spirit that I was a stumbling block to His will in her life. I needed to obey Him and send her. I prayed for my daughter and filled out the form. I was truly being moved by the Spirit of God, because I knew my own spirit was revolting.

Since my daughter was only sixteen at the time, I made arrangements to fly to Montana with her. This was her first flight, and because she was young, I was not about to put her on a plane without me! (I guess my faith wasn't that strong after all.) We totally enjoyed our flight out there, and we looked forward to seeing what Montana looked like. We were amazed at its beauty.

Montana is so unlike Virginia; yet it had a beauty all its own. After getting our rental car at the airport, Ashleigh and I headed to the nearest Five Guys, got lunch, and headed for the YWAM base. We were mesmerized by the mountains that surrounded us along with the very flat highway we traveled. It was truly picturesque. I had a hard time keeping the car on the road; I just couldn't take my eyes off the mountains. Miraculously, in spite of my poor driving and directional skills, we arrived at the base!

The base itself was set in a valley of trees and shared access to a beautiful lake nearby. The place was quiet and serene—and a bit creepy. We parked in the parking lot, walked to the office, and tried to find a person to help us get Ashleigh checked in and find her room. There was no help at the office, it was empty of people. The base itself was not attractive. It was an old military base and needed some redecorating. This first appearance began an uneasy feeling in

Ashleigh and me. I tried to hide my feelings of anxiety and instead be confident that God had a plan for my daughter in this strange-looking place.

We finally found the person in charge, and she showed Ashleigh her room. She was very friendly, and her welcoming aura helped put us at ease. We unpacked and noticed a note written to Ashleigh by one of the staff members whom she had not met yet. Each staff member was given a name of a YWAM camper; they were to write a note of encouragement to each and welcome them as they arrived. The note brought us both to tears and gave us confirmation that Ashleigh was indeed meant to be there. I don't remember the note word for word, but I do remember two things that stood out to us.

Dear Ashleigh,

Each YWAM staff member was asked to pick a camper and pray over them before their arrival. And I picked your name. I have been praying for you.

God gave me one word for you: <u>strength.</u> I know that God will strengthen your faith as you spend the next two months with us.

He also gave me a verse just for you, and that verse is Isaiah 61:1-3, "The Spirit of the Lord GOD is upon me, because the LORD has anointed me to bring good news to the afflicted; He has sent me to bind up the brokenhearted, to proclaim liberty to captives and freedom to prisoners; to proclaim the favorable year of the LORD and the day of vengeance of our God; to comfort all who mourn, to grant those

*who mourn in Zion, giving them a garland
instead of ashes, the oil of gladness instead of
mourning, the mantle of praise instead of a
spirit of fainting. So they will be called oaks of
righteousness, the planting of the LORD, that
He may be glorified."*

As tears streamed down our faces, we both came to the conclusion that God's hand was upon this mission for Ashleigh, regardless of how creepy the place seemed to us.

Many years ago, when my family was very young, I had an impression from God during a church service. He impressed upon me a very specific purpose for each of my children. My first, Matthew, was born for the purposes of leadership. Ashleigh was born for the purpose of strength. Nick, was born for hope, and Scott was born to bring me closer to the Lord in ways I do not know yet. I don't understand that last one, but I do know that one day, I will. That's almost scary, because I have no idea what will come my way in this new revelation of God for me. The word *strength* lighted the note for me, as it brought me back to that day when God struck my heart with His plans for my children. Ashleigh is living that purpose in her life. I have seen her be strong for her family and friends.

When Ashleigh looked at the verse the young woman chose for her, she looked up at me and said, "Mom, this is the very passage of Scripture I have made as my life verse." We hugged, cried, and praised the Lord for His unfailing comfort in this new environment we initially felt unsure about.

After getting Ashleigh settled and meeting other campers, we reclined for a time in a room the base allowed me to stay in until the following morning. For several weeks before we arrived in Montana, we had studied the subject of love in the Bible together; we decided that we would conclude our time that evening continuing in our study and praying for her mission. We cried some more, as we both knew that we already missed each other. Stepping out in faith was hard to do, and letting God hold my daughter in His hands took all the faith I had.

Finally, Ashleigh and I walked back to her room and visited a little longer. Then I left and went to my room. I cried all night long. I prayed for God to protect her and bring her back to me safely. Sending our children on missions brings us one step closer to believing that God is real and that His hands are stronger and even more faithful than our own.

Finally, I woke at 5:30 a.m. I packed my bags, put them in the rental car, and went to Ashleigh's room to see her one more time. She was sound asleep, and I chose not to wake her. Instead, I laid my hands on her and prayed for her. I could barely see through my tears. Suddenly, I could not leave the room, even though I knew I had to. I had a plane to catch, but I feared I would scoop her up and take her back home with me. I wanted to. I silently prayed, *Holy Spirit, move my body through the door, into the car, and drive me to the airport, because my flesh is not moving.* He did just that. This time in my life was a faith-builder for me and Ashleigh. I will never forget it. My faith in God became knowledge that my God is faithful.

I arrived at the airport with swollen eyes. I continued crying as I sat in my seat on the plane. I reflected on my experience of sending my daughter on a mission and remembered Hannah in 1 Samuel 1–2. Hannah was the wife of Elkanah. Elkanah had two wives, Peninnah and Hannah. Penninnah had children, but Hannah had none. Hannah wanted to have children. It was her heart's desire, as was true of all Jewish women. It was the goal in life for a woman to bear her husband children. Hannah's days were filled with weeping and not eating; she was so distressed over not having children that her husband was greatly concerned for her. He said to her, "Hannah, why are you weeping? Why don't you eat? Why are you downhearted? Don't I mean more to you than ten sons?" (1 Samuel 1:8)

Feeling defeated, Hannah went to the house of the Lord and cried out to Him. Her prayer to God came from a deeper place than her heart; it was a plea from her very soul. Her tears were the result of her great love for her child whom she had not yet received. However, her love for her God was far greater than even her love for her child. When she beseeched the Lord for a son, her prayer had God's purposes as the focus.

Hannah made a vow: "Lord Almighty, if you will only look on your servant's misery and remember me, and not forget your servant but give her a son, then I will give him to the Lord for all the days of his life" (1 Samuel 1:11). She knew that God would not only hear her, but also answer her. We see her confidence in God's provision. After praying, "She went her way and ate something, and her face was no longer downcast" (1 Samuel 1:18). As I sat on the plane, I knew that God would take care of my daughter. I could trust Him to be faithful to His promise.

Hannah did give birth to a son named, Samuel. She nursed him until he was three years old, and Hannah was true to her vow. She took her little boy and dedicated him to a life of service to the Lord at the temple. Samuel lived with Eli and his sons. At the temple, Samuel heard from the Lord and eventually became one of the greatest godly influences Israel ever had.

It is important to take note of the other wife in this story. Peninnah had children by Elkanah, but her character was ugly. All we hear about this woman is that she taunted Hannah for not having children.

We know that she had sons and daughters. God does not paint a very pretty picture of this woman. Even her husband loved Hannah more than Peninnah. In the end, we never hear how her children impacted the world. We never see her children influence anyone or anything. We only hear of Samuel, his love for God, and his influence on the nation of Israel.

I love how Hannah describes herself and Peninnah in her prayer of praise to the Lord after taking Samuel to the house of God: "Those who were well fed are now starving; and those who were starving are now full. The barren woman now has seven children; but the woman with many children will have no more" (1 Samuel 2:5).

This speaks beyond just giving birth to children; it speaks of a child's continued influence beyond the womb and beyond the family boundaries. Having children and raising them for this world leaves us empty. However, having children and raising them for God's purposes and His will continues to fill the Lord's cup with overflowing blessings. Peninnah's glory ended with her ugly character, while Hannah's influence lived on through Samuel.

Samuel was the bridge between the judges and the kings. He was the one who anointed Saul as the first King of Israel and later anointed David as the second King of Israel. David, the man after God's own heart, was also in the line that Jesus would eventually come from.

Samuel was wise and obedient to God's Word. He was firm and stood fast against the evil deeds of King Saul. He spoke truth and did not flinch in the face of opposition. As a result, Samuel's example of influence lives on. What would have happened if Hannah had not dedicated Samuel to the Lord? What if she selfishly hoarded her son all to herself? The what-ifs are good to reflect on, because they help us realize that our decisions can alter humankind. What if Eve had said *no* to the serpent? Where would we as a human race be in our relationship to sin and ultimately to the Father?

This is why it is imperative that we dedicate our children to the Lord. We give them to Him for *His* purposes. His purpose reigns forever; through God, our children's acts of righteousness will continue to bless others forever if we choose the right path to follow in parenting. As Ralph Waldo Emerson says, "The best efforts of a fine person [are] felt after we have left their presence."

Upon Ashleigh's return, my family celebrated her freedom and the mission that God sent her on. She shared with us all the people who came to Christ in Germany. She taught us how to do open-air outreach so we could continue this in our little town in Virginia. She brought a heart for ministry and an aim to fulfill God's will everywhere she went. She has been able to use all that God taught her on this mission to continue ministry at home and in her future.

Jesus said to his disciples, "The harvest is plentiful, but the workers are few. Ask the Lord of the harvest, therefore, to send out workers into His harvest field" (Luke 10:2). The church often uses this passage when seeking volunteers for ministry. My challenge is to parents, not the church. This verse says that the harvest is plentiful, meaning that the opportunities for serving the lost and hurting are ample. In addition to this, we need to see that the workers are few.

The workers are not few because they don't exist; they are few because the workers reside in the cocoon and are not allowed to blossom into the beautiful butterflies of blessings they are meant to be. Parents hold their children back today by keeping them immature, coddled, and weak. This leads me to the question, "How can parents prepare their children for the harvest?"

Mature the Immature

We live in a culture that promotes and even elevates the teenage years as if they mark the end of growing up. One of the ways we see this is in the comments made by parents. "Teenagers will be teenagers." "Teenagers are just having fun." "They will grow out of this stage." "Let them be kids."

The problem with this mindset is that if you raise them to be teenagers, they will remain teenagers. A good definition for *teenage years* today is a time in children's lives when maturity is delayed so they can be allowed to do stupid things that corrupt their ability to be complete, responsible individuals who bless society.

There is no concept of teenage years in the Bible. At age twelve or thirteen, young girls were ready to be married and learn how to run a home, raise a family, and help their husbands. Young boys of ages twelve and thirteen were ready for the Rabbinical school (our form of higher education) and beginning the rigors of a trade. God knew well that the teenage years were not a profitable stopping stage for children. Making the teenage years the ending point only keeps them immature.

I have often told my children when they became thirteen years old, they are not teenagers; they are young adults. This is key to their preparation for mission work or even allowing them to move out of the home.

One of the best ways you can determine if your child has developed the kind of maturity he or she needs to move out from your daily influence is to see whether he or she currently values your advice and direction. If your child truly seeks the leadership of his or her elders and follows through on the guidance given, then he or she has developed incredible maturity. You can trust that your child will go out on his or her own, actually obey what he or she is told, and grow from the instructions given.

This doesn't mean your teen will always agree with you when you direct him or her; it means your teen is willing to trust you regardless of his or her own small sphere of perspective. Your child has the humility it takes to see himself or herself as inexperienced and in need of reliance on his or her seniors for a broader viewpoint.

A trusting relationship with your child makes this possible. The way to develop trust with your young adult is to have a track record with him or her of your own faithfulness in his or her life. When children don't agree with our decisions for them, if they are not happy with the direction we take them, or if they assume we are just being spiteful, there are questions you can ask that help them gain perspective.

Try the question, "Do you think I woke up this morning and planned to make your life miserable?" Your children know that this is not true. Another question to ask them is, "Do you think I do the things I do for you because I love you or because I have to?" Try asking, "Is there a time in your life where I made a decision for you for the sole purpose of tormenting you?" If you have a thinking child who can answer these questions with "Of course not," then you have an open door to influence him or her in a positive way.

Remember to tell your children that all of life is not explainable. The one thing we can trust is God's Word. With that trust, we can follow Him in total obedience. Explain that there have been many times when God has asked you to obey Him in areas that you did not understand. The only thing you had to do was trust in who He was. You did not have to understand what He was asking. The same is true in their response to their elders. If they are sure of their elders' and parents' love for them and genuine concern for their welfare, then they can trust the advice or direction given based on who they are, not what they have decided.

The minute a child is born, parents begin the process of teaching him or her to be independent. Each step he or she takes is toward maturity. There should never be a delay in this process. Delays on our part are simply stumbling blocks we need to remove. Maturity starts when children are young and moves seamlessly into their young adulthood.

If your child can make a bed, then he should make his own bed. If a child can do dishes, then she can take part in that family chore. If your teen can read and write, then he can read and fill out his own college application. If your young adult can type, then she can develop her own resume for a job. Will your child need assistance at first? Absolutely! Will he or she fail at times? Yes, indeed! Will your child learn? If we allow our children to learn, then they will.

Do Not Coddle

Coddling our children includes pampering and spoiling them. It is natural for a parent to want to protect his or her child from fears and hurts, but if this is taken to a level of enabling him or her to be dependent on the parent, coddling actually weakens the child's ability to stand firm.

Let's be real, life is filled with disappointments, failures, and difficulties. We cannot escape this; nor can our children. They have to walk the same walk we have walked. This walk only strengthens their resolve to press on when life is hard. If parents have truly taken to heart raising their children for the Lord, teaching them His truth, and pointing them to His strength, then children will learn in the midst of struggles to stand firm. Sometimes the best way to help them stand firm is to let them fail.

My son, Matt, has allowed me to share one of his not-so-successful situations. He graduated from home school high school at age eighteen with a GPA of 3.2. He loves God and is an all-around responsible individual who you can count on. He is faithful to his commitments, easygoing, and a fun person to be around. However, his first two years of college were challenging. His first year was a semi-success, but his second year was a complete failure.

Matt struggled with wanting to even be in college. He wasn't sure what direction he wanted to take; therefore, he simply did not apply himself. I encouraged him and warned him that his lack of application to his college classes would one day come back to haunt him. He did not listen and failed every class that second year of college. I let him fail. I knew that the best way for him to learn was from his mistakes not just my advice.

Allowing failure is often a part of the process of letting our children grow. In the end, Matt did learn that his mistakes were the result of his poor choices that year. When he finally wanted to do something with his life and discovered the college he ultimately wanted to go to, he was not accepted because of that one year of failed classes. It brought his grade point average below the accepted requirement. He was deflated but motivated to do something about it.

Matt has worked to get his grades up so he could be accepted to this college. He is still working toward his goal, but this time, he is working for himself, not because his parents want it.

Raising independent children starts when they are young. Not purchasing everything they want and not giving them everything they desire are two actions that can be taken. Make your children work for their electronics, and teach them to value what the dollar can buy. Don't just give them what they want; give them the value needed to care for what they want. Likewise, allowing them to fail and experience the consequences teaches them to take responsibility for their lives. It was quite painful for me to allow Matt to fail his second year of college, but my goal was to see my son develop into a man, not remain a boy.

I have learned that it is important to keep this rule of thumb in mind: if my child can do something, I should let him or her do it. It is not easy, but if applied, it is a powerful tool in our children's hands. Nothing builds more confidence and character than being independent and being able to stand firm on our own two feet. We know this as adults, so why would we rob this from our children?

It is just as important to walk with our young adult children. Leaving them stranded and abandoned is not allowing them to stand firm. Keeping in touch with them and assisting them where they need true assistance is important. Paul instructs parents in Ephesians 6:4, "...do not exasperate your children."

When our children struggle, we need to come alongside them and help them in ways that keep them going forward. I discovered that working a part-time job and going to school actually inhibited Matt's ability to do well in school, so his father and I agreed that he should not work and throw himself fully into his schoolwork. This has worked, and he is able to focus entirely on his school load and bring up those grades. We figured that if allowing him to be supported financially during this time of his life ultimately helped him do well in school, it also moved him forward to complete independence when he moved out on his own.

It is never good to cause our children despair. Our goal is to strengthen the will of God in our children. Keeping that goal in mind will help us strike the balance needed to fulfill His vision for our children.

Strengthen Feeble Arms and Weak Knees

One of our goals in raising our children is to produce strong character and reward accomplishment. Children will rise to our expectations, whether they are good or bad.

For example, a mom said to her daughter, "If you want to be sexually active, let me know so I can get you birth control pills." The mom's expectation was that her daughter would indeed become sexually active. Presented with this expectation in the form of suggestion, her daughter did become sexually active.

What if this mom reworded this expectation in a different manner? "If you are tempted to be sexually active, let's look at what God says about the consequences of being sexually immoral and how He can give you self-control." The expectation here is that when temptation comes your way, God can give you the strength to overcome the temptation so you can remain pure.

The first expectation plunges the girl into defeat; the other embraces victory. Which do you think would enable the young girl to develop self-respect? The second expectation, of course.

The expectations parents set for their children will either strengthen or weaken them. Our expectations will depend on our ultimate goal for our children. One of my goals for my children is sexual purity. I believe that they each can maintain virginity until marriage. While I am discussing this one goal as an example, keep in mind that we can apply the elements I mention to any goal we set for our children.

When we set expectations, they include the following elements: discussion, boundaries, recovery, and review.

Discussion Gives Clarity

Parents either discuss sex with their children or run from it altogether. If you are going to set an expectation for sexual purity with your children, you need to make this an open conversation with them! This cannot be a secret or a taboo topic in the home. It can be embarrassing, but I encourage you to get over your embarrassment and give your children the wisdom they need in this area. Don't be afraid of something beautiful that God created. If you neglect speaking to your children about this creation of God, you can count on them learning about it through the filthy lens of culture.

Allow your children to ask questions, and answer them. If it helps, be scientific about it. Reply to their questions with short, succinct answers. At many different ages, your children will bring you questions on this topic. Be willing to stop and talk about their questions; this open communication expresses clarity for them. In this discussion, it is important to set the boundaries of what you expect for and from them.

Boundaries Give Direction

Boundaries give our children clear direction and obtainable tasks to accomplish. With my goal for sexual purity, an example of a boundary would be, *don't be alone with the opposite sex, be in groups so temptation is minimal, and only give side hugs.*

It is also important to create these boundaries *with* your children; you won't agree with all of their ideas, but working together gives them a say and opportunity to explain their point of view. At the end of this discussion and boundary-setting, you will ultimately set the standard. Children appreciate the fact they were respected enough to participate in the planning. This is especially true for teenagers.

Clarity and direction help children reach success when an expectation is given. They are also measurable. Measurability is very important to children; without it, they feel insecure about the target they trying to obey.

Recovery from Failure Gives Hope

When the boundaries are crossed—and at times, they will be—it is time for another discussion. Confession, reiterating the expectation, and reviewing the boundaries are necessary.

Just because a parent has set an expectation doesn't mean a child won't cross it. Unfortunately, I have seen a child cross the boundary and parents end up lowering the expectation instead of tightening the boundary.

A parent set the expectation for her daughter to not be sexually active, and then the young girl crossed the boundary. She did not have sex, but she crossed the boundary of being alone with a boy and kissing him rather passionately. A parent who lowers the boundary is one who says, "Well, at least they didn't have sex. Teens will be teens." Immediately, this expectation was lowered. This young girl will cross this boundary and many more.

Another approach would be to tighten the boundary to supervision of the girl with her friends for a time until she succeeds at understanding the value of self-control. A repentant heart also needs to be encouraged before privileges are given back. This could take some time, but it encourages the girl to see that she has work to do in order to have victory in achieving the set expectation. In the end, this tightening of the boundary will give her ultimate success and hope for a second chance.

Reviewing the Expectation Gives Solidity

Reviewing the expectation often is a practice that solidifies a child's success in keeping it strong. On the subject of sexual purity, there are many ways to keep this expectation fresh.

Read books with your teen on the topic. Attend special conferences on sexual purity. Have your teen join accountability groups at church, give him or her sermons specific to this topic to listen to, and even share examples of teens who have not kept the boundary and their consequences. You will notice that all of these require parent involvement. In any expectation set for children, parents need to be involved, and they need to be specific about what is required. This requires an on-going relationship that encourages questions and further exploration.

I used sexual purity as an example of an expectation. Nonetheless, the steps I used of discussion, boundaries, recovering from failure, and review can be applied to all expectations we set for our children. Strong godly expectations demand discipline and produce strong young adults.

Hebrews 12:12–13 gives us a reason to develop strong young adults. "Take a new grip with your tired hands and stand firm on your shaky legs. Mark out a straight path for your feet. Then those who follow you, though they are weak and lame, will not stumble and fall but will become strong."

The key phrase in this passage is "those who follow you." Our children follow us, and someone follows them. In order for our children to be wide in influence, we need to strengthen their feeble hands and weak knees by giving them godly expectations and effective accomplishments that will propel the kingdom of God forth with power.

If you have led your children with weakness, then take a new grip; mark out a straight path for your feet. Begin a new way to lead them. You can do it, because God is here to change us forward, not leave us behind in our muck of mistakes.

Parenting is hard work indeed. Some of us walk harder roads

than others. I don't ever want to take your situation and speak of it lightly. I certainly could have suffered more in my parenting journey. Some face mountains I can't even imagine facing. Some may wonder how on earth they can overcome the mistakes they've made or the walls they climb. I don't belittle your experience, but I do applaud the power of our God to help you overcome anything you face.

The lyrics to "Press On" by Selah have encouraged me on my journey. Read them, and feel the Lord lift you under His wings in refuge, strength, and power.

When the valley is deep,
When the mountain is steep,
When the body is weary,
When we stumble and fall,

When the choices are hard,
When we're battered and scarred,
When we've spent our resources,
When we've given our all,

In Jesus' name, we press on.
In Jesus' name, we press on.

Dear Lord, with the prize
Clear before our eyes,
We find the strength to press on.

In Jesus' name, we press on.
In Jesus' name, we press on.

Dear Lord, with the prize
Clear before our eyes,

We find the strength to press on—
To press on.

Reflection and Review

1. Read about Hannah in 1 Samuel 1:1–20. Describe her desire for a child and what it might have felt like to drop him off at the temple at age three.
2. What challenges do you face in sending your child out? How can God strengthen you?
3. How can parents prepare their children for the harvest?
4. Take an expectation for your child, and describe ways you can turn this into an expectation that honors God.
5. What expectations have you lowered for your children because of their failures? How can you tighten them so your children can succeed?
6. In what ways do the lyrics to "Press On" by Selah encourage you?

Closing Challenge

We live in a hard-hearted culture. I echo what Jesus said to his disciples: "The harvest is plentiful but the workers are few" (Matthew 9:37). We can also say that the people are plentiful, but the faithful are few. I am not speaking to the lost in our culture but to those who claim salvation. There appear to be many people who claim a relationship with Jesus in our churches; yet few truly seek God with repentance, humility, and obedience. Going through the motions is their way of life. But God wants us to go to Him, seeking His favor and His blessing. We can't obtain His favor with calloused hearts for Him.

King Josiah of Judah, the grandson of King Manasseh, led the nation of Israel in a reformation. He destroyed the gods that his grandfather had set up and reinstated the temple and worship to God. He did great things for the people of Judah, who had lived fifty-five years in the midst of the worst evil the nation had ever encountered under King Manasseh's reign. Yet even though King Josiah humbled himself before God, the people simply followed orders of behavior. They did not experience a genuine change of their hearts. Their hearts became so hard toward God's law and His ways they did not fully turn back to Him. Unfortunately, when King Josiah died, they returned to their wicked ways. Their rebellion brought God's judgment upon them.

Believe it or not, we live in a similar hard-hearted culture. The battle for our children's souls is on and has been going on since the time of Adam and Eve. However, in these latter days, the intensity of the battle is already beginning the process of segregating the goats from the sheep and the weeds from the wheat. There are a lot more dead churches in communities than there are ones alive for Christ. Though a church may have high attendance, you have to find the reason for these large numbers before entrusting your soul to its leading. Growth in numbers is not always a sign of upholding the Word of God and obedience to Him. It can often mean the church meets a need for cultural fulfillment and personal purpose. It is not necessarily for the glory of God.

The reason I say the battle segregates the goats from the sheep is because the hard-hearted culture is now in our churches, not just in the lost people in our society. Church use to be a place you could go and trust the leadership to be faithful to the Word of God. It was a place where you could find unity in morality and faith. Now the church has become part of the battleground. This is why parents cannot just sanction the spiritual responsibility to the church.

Yes, there are good churches in our country, but they are few and becoming fewer—not fewer in number but fewer in sheep. I certainly do not recommend that you stop attending church, but don't leave the spiritual education of your children only to the church. Children need this to come from their parents.

There are many pastors and ministers today who can't handle the battle, and they give up and return to secular vocations, leaving the sheep unattended and uncared for. Giving up is easy and even understandable. When the heat is hotter, we want to run, not burn. This is the same with raising children. When raising them is hard and we find less energy, passion, and vision for bringing them to Jesus, many parents will give up. They give their children over to the culture. They hope for the best, and sadly, their children often times experience the worst.

I challenge you to *not give up!* Jeremiah, the prophet, was to communicate the Word of God to a hard-hearted culture. His assignment taxed his spirit, tested his faith, tried his patience, and demanded physical stamina. God told Jeremiah,

> Get yourself ready! Stand up and say to them (the Kings of Judah, its officials, its priests, and the people of the land) whatever I say to you. Do not be terrified by them, or I will terrify you before them. Today, I have made you a fortified city, an iron pillar and a bronze wall to stand against the whole land. They will fight against you but will not overcome you, for I am with you and will rescue you. (Jeremiah 1:17–19)

We glean a promise from the Lord in His words to Jeremiah. Yes, parenting our children is hard, and spiritually training them in a hard culture seems impossible. But God is with you! He will rescue you! He will speak through you! You can count on winning, because what seems impossible to humans is not impossible for Him.

God promises, "I am watching over My word to perform it" (Jeremiah 1:12). He also encourages us that His purpose will stand, and He will do all that He pleases (Isaiah 46:10b). His promises are sure, and we can trust in Him, even in our old age. He is God, and He will sustain us. He has made us, and He will carry us. He not only sustains us, but also rescues us (Isaiah 46:4).

We can also be assured that when God's Word is spoken and delivered to our children, He has an eternal purpose to accomplish in those words. His Word that goes out from His mouth will not return to Him empty; it will accomplish what He desires and achieve the purpose for which He sent it (Isaiah 55:11). As parents to our children, will we choose to be His faithful sheep or His retreating goats?

God goes on to tell us that His eyes "range throughout the earth to strengthen those whose hearts are fully committed to Him" (1

Chronicles 16:9). King Josiah made the wonderful decision to humble himself before the Lord, but he lost the battle in changing the hearts of the people of Judah. Their calloused hearts mocked God. We don't want to follow King Josiah's failure. Yes, we need to be victorious over our own sin and find salvation for our souls before we give it to our children. But this is not the end of the road.

Many God-fearing parents raise God-defying children. Take this salvation that God has given you one step further and give it to your children with planning, prayer, and persistence. I believe what Jesus says in Matthew 22:10: "He who stands firm to the end will be saved." This doesn't mean eternal life; it means preservation. If we persevere and stand firm in our commitment to give our children His Word and disciple them in His truth, God will preserve our efforts in our children. He will accomplish His desires for them. If we delight ourselves in Him, I know He will confirm his promise to us. He will give us the desires of our hearts (Psalm 37:4).

When my children were very young, I used to lay my hands on them while they were asleep and pray over their souls. I prayed for God to draw them to Himself and for each to be assured of His love. I prayed for each to grow up with a hunger for His truth and a desire to serve Him with all his or her heart and life.

After praying for my children one evening, I began to truly pray for myself and my husband. I knew that this prayer could not be fully answered unless God was truly changing us for His glory and purposes. In the quiet of this moment, I felt the hand of the Spirit of God upon me, and I wrote a poem. It was more of a prayer to my God than a piece of literature. It was my heart's desire, and I wanted to see this desire to completion. I knew that the good work God began in me would see its end in His perfect power. But I was still moved to articulate my heart on paper.

Before the Lord, I Stood

My time will come
When I'm before the Lord;
He'll speak to me
With His powerful Word.

He'll judge my days
That I spent with my child;
He'll ask me of my time
As each moment was filed.

"I gave you a child,"
He'll say to me.
"Did you teach him well?
Did you help him see?"

"Did you read him my Word?"
The Lord will ask.
"Or was it myths and legends
That burdened your task?"

"Did you show him my steps?"
The Lord will pry.
"Or was it man's glory
That touched his cry?"

"Did you show him I'm infallible?"
The Lord will inquire.
"Or was it man's competency
That filled his desire?"

"Did you teach him My ways?"
The Lord will say.
"Or was it the path of man
That led his way?"

"Did you show him my compassion?"
I could feel the Lord's presence.
"Or was it the pride and riches of man
That defiled his essence?"

My time will come.
What will I say, and what will I tell?
The longing of my heart is to respond,
"O Lord, I taught him; I taught him well."

My Prayer for You

While we have concluded this book, we have not concluded our journey. Our journey of parenting began when we received Christ and continued when God gifted us with little disciples in our quiver. My prayer for you is that you will love your quiver with our heavenly Father's heart.

Dear God,

I am glad for the challenges you give me as a parent and as spokesperson in Your name, for I am completing Your calling and fulfilling Your will for Your people. You have given me as well as every parent reading this book the responsibility of serving our children by proclaiming Your message in all its fullness to them.

This message was kept secret for centuries and generations past, but now it is revealed to Your people. It pleases You, God, for us to tell our children of Your riches and glory in Christ. Your desire is for none of our children to perish but for all to live forever in Christ. Your Son is our assurance that we all will share in His glory.

Wherever we go, may we be driven by Your love to tell our children of Christ, warn them of sin and Satan's schemes, and teach them with all the wisdom You have given us, for we want to present each of our children to You as perfect in their relationship with Christ.

We do this very hard work, as we each depend on Christ's mighty power that works within us. May our children be taught by the Lord so they will have immense peace with You. Give each parent reading this book a new vision in his or her role to his or her children; give each parent renewed passion in his or her relationship with You and his or her children so that together, they will impact this world and draw all people to You with Your amazing love!

In Jesus' holy name, amen.

Thank you for reading this book. May it bless you as you reach out to your children with the love of God. I love you all! I may not know you by name, but I pray for the parents of this culture and for their children.

Endnotes

1   *The Strongest NASB Exhaustive Concordance* (Grand Rapids: Zondervan, 2000), Hebrew Reference Number 3824.

Chapter Three
2   Sandy Dengler, *Susanna Wesley, Servant of God* (Chicago: The Moody Bible Institute, 1987), 46.
3   Ibid, 64.

Chapter Six
4   Ibid, 165.
5   *The Strongest NASB Exhaustive Concordance* (Grand Rapids: Zondervan, 2000), Hebrew Reference Number 8150.
6   Kathleen White, *Amy Carmichael* (Minneapolis: Bethany House Publishers, 1986), 50.
7   John C. Maxwell, *The 21 Indispensable Qualities of a Leader* (Nashville: Thomas Nelson, Inc., 1999), 133.
8   Ibid, 13.

About the Author

Marcie Cramsey has a zeal for helping parents surrender their lives to God, and out of that relationship, raise devoted followers of Christ. She currently holds the position of Children's Minister at Fairview at River Club and has been in ministry to families and children for more than twenty-five years. She is married to her husband of twenty-seven years; together, they have three sons, one daughter, and one son-in-law. They reside in Culpeper, Virginia.

CPSIA information can be obtained at www.ICGtesting.com
Printed in the USA
BVOW000106010513

319542BV00002B/213/P